ASLEEP
IN
DIRT

photographs by
Yair Oelbaum

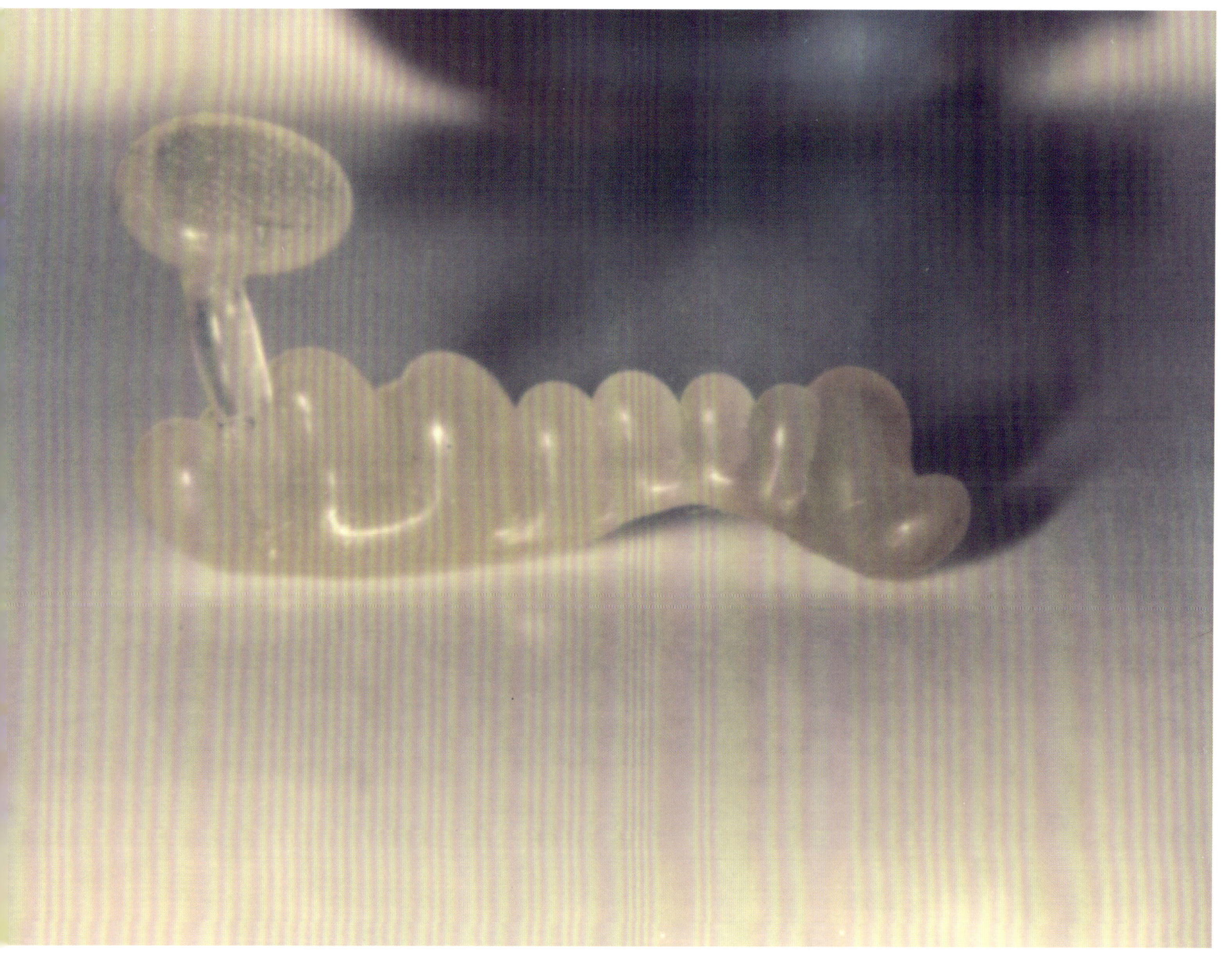

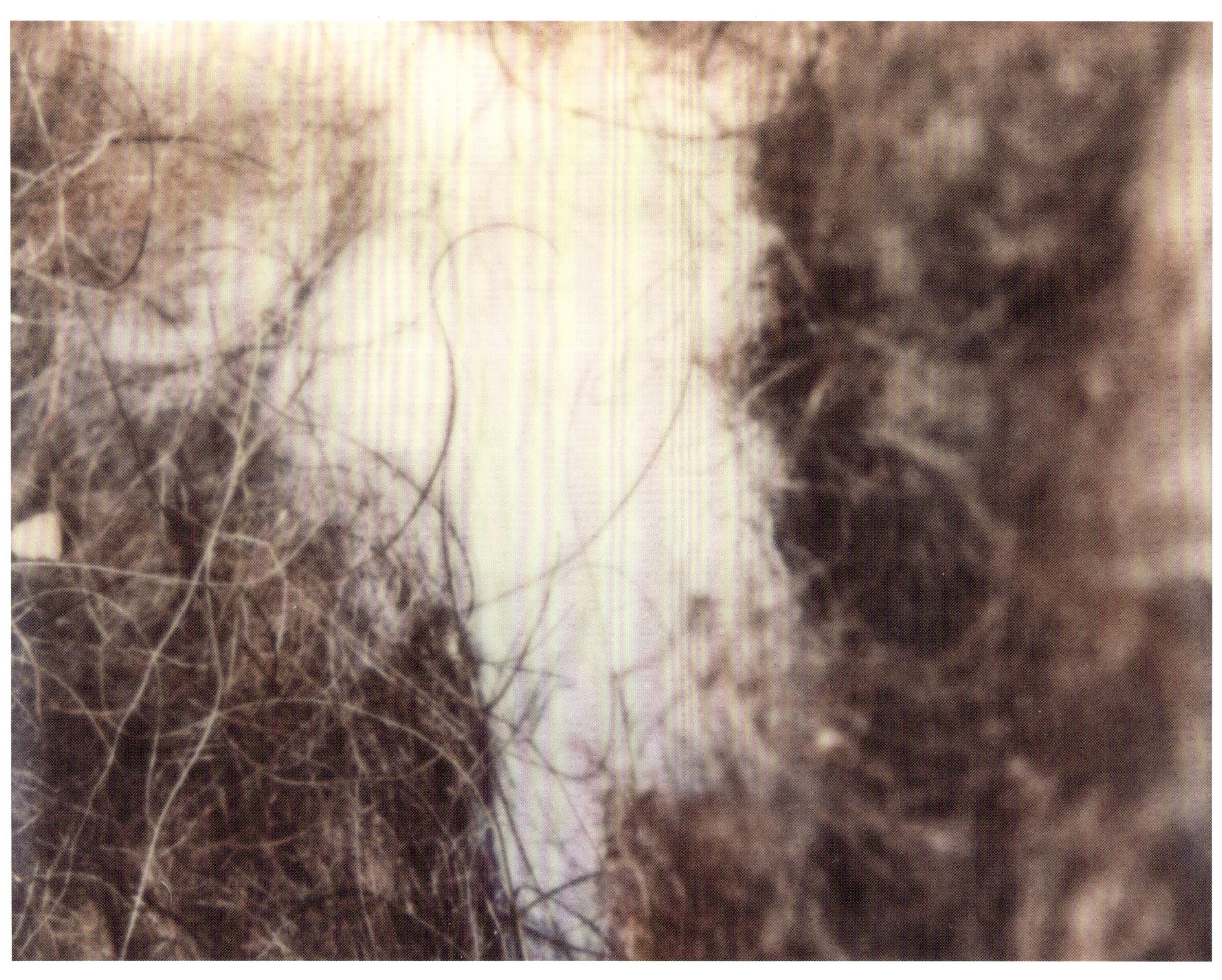

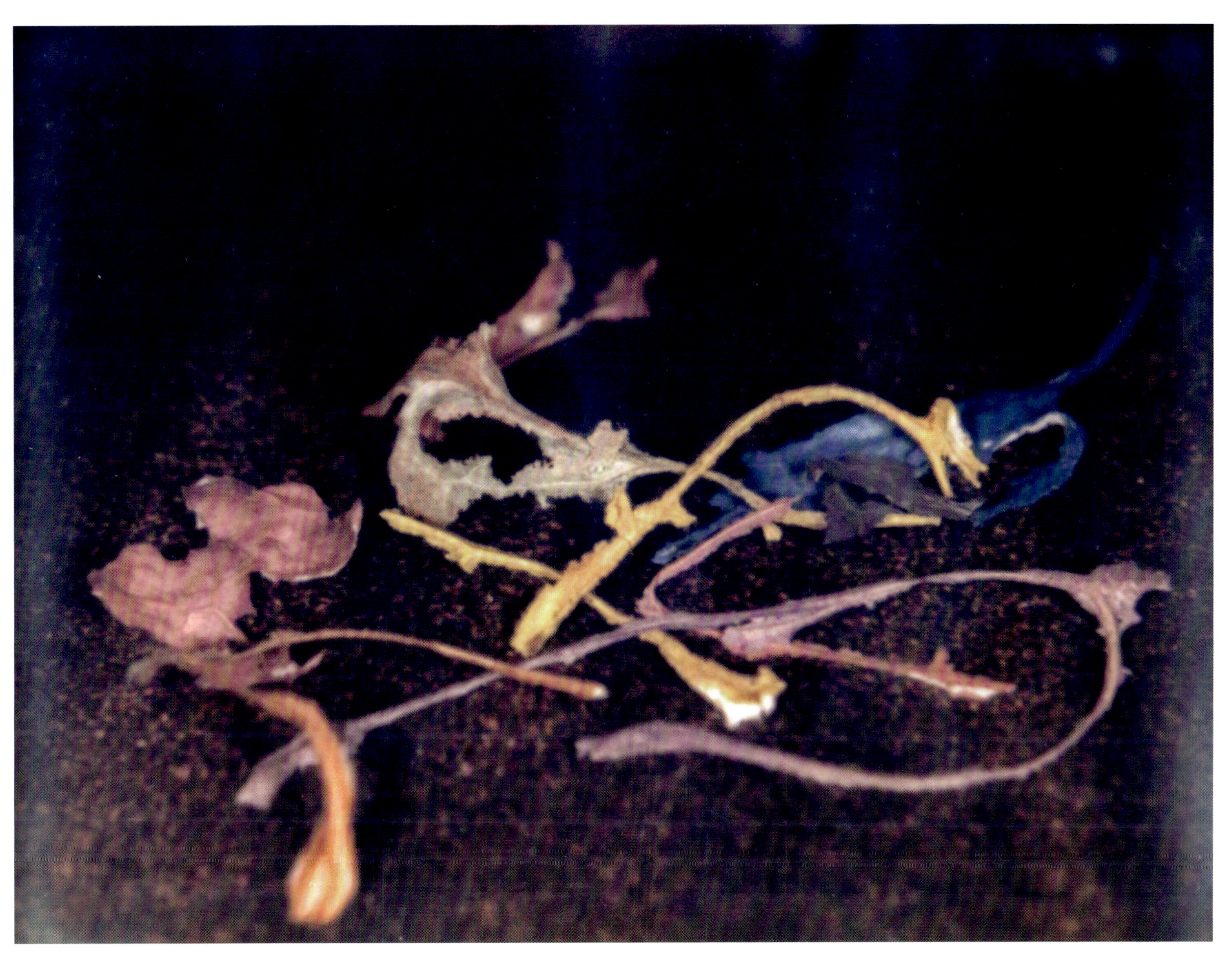

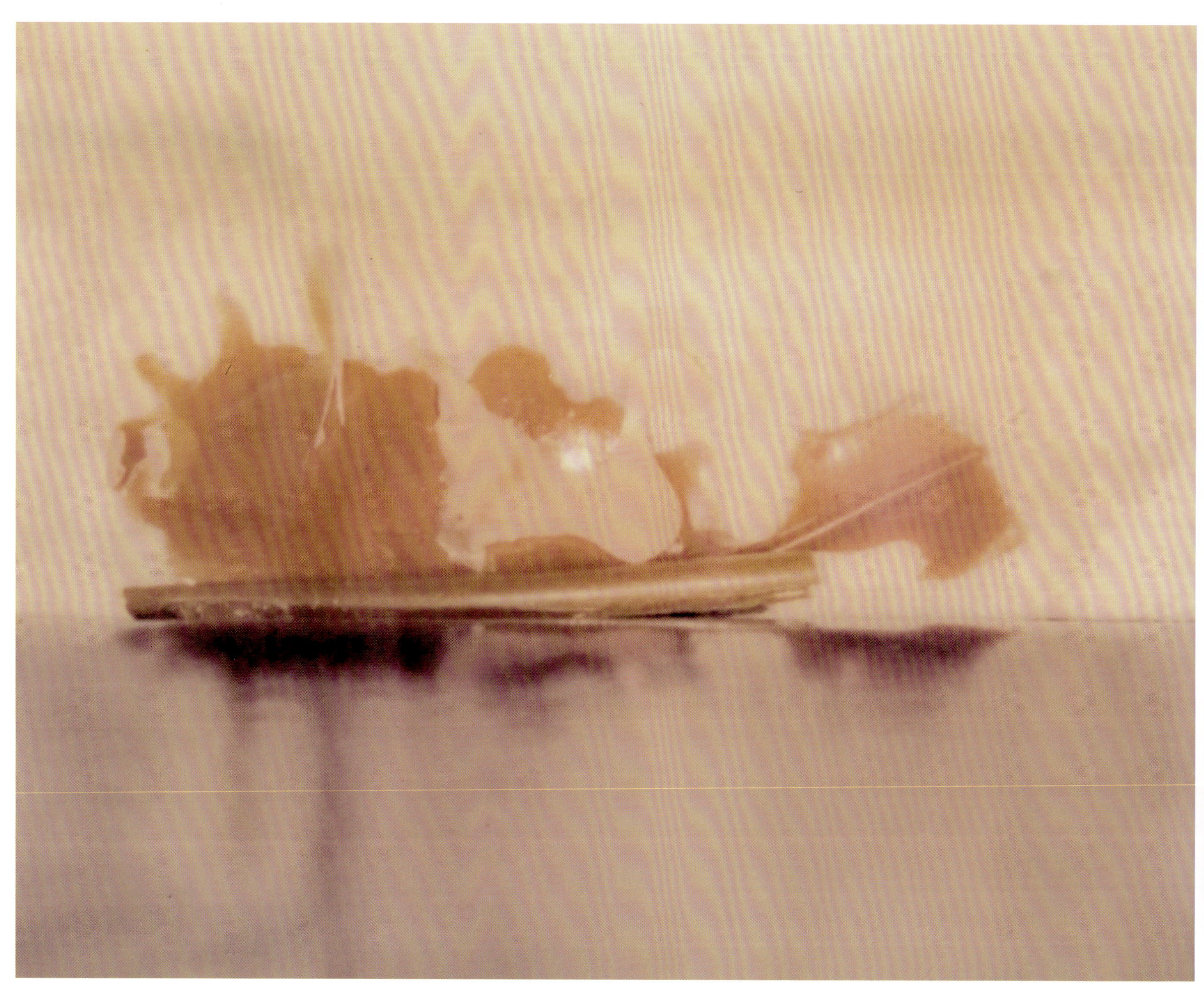

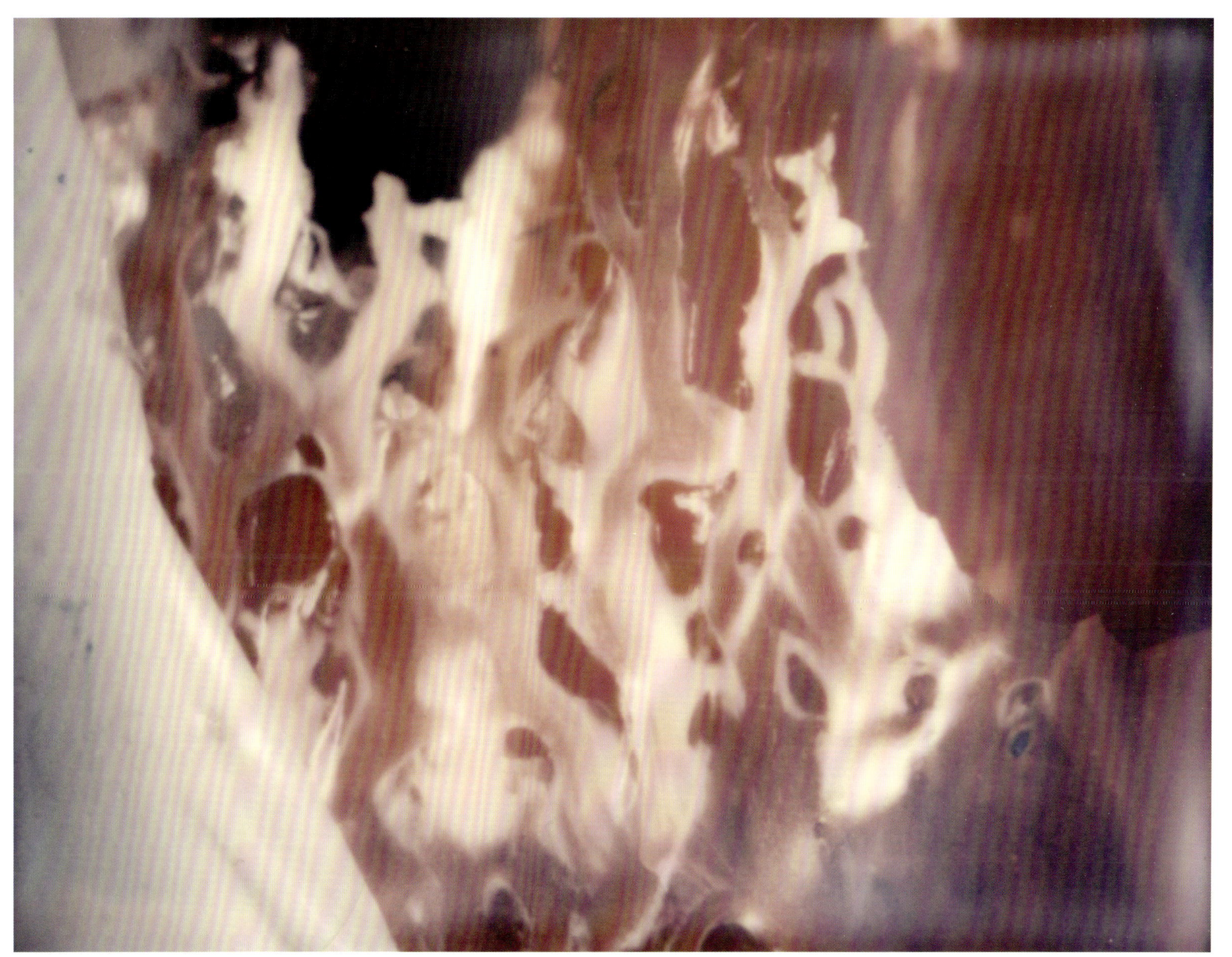

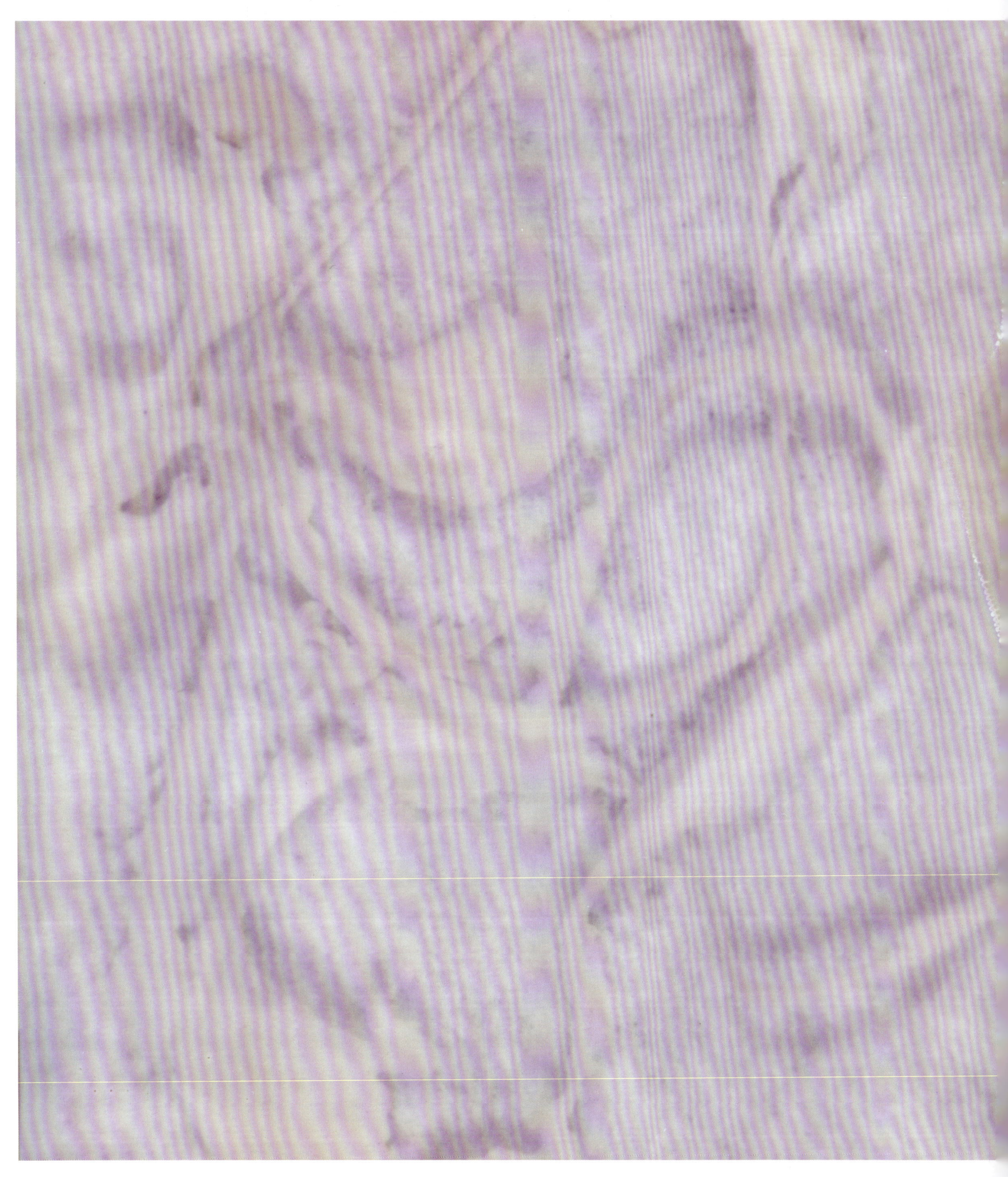

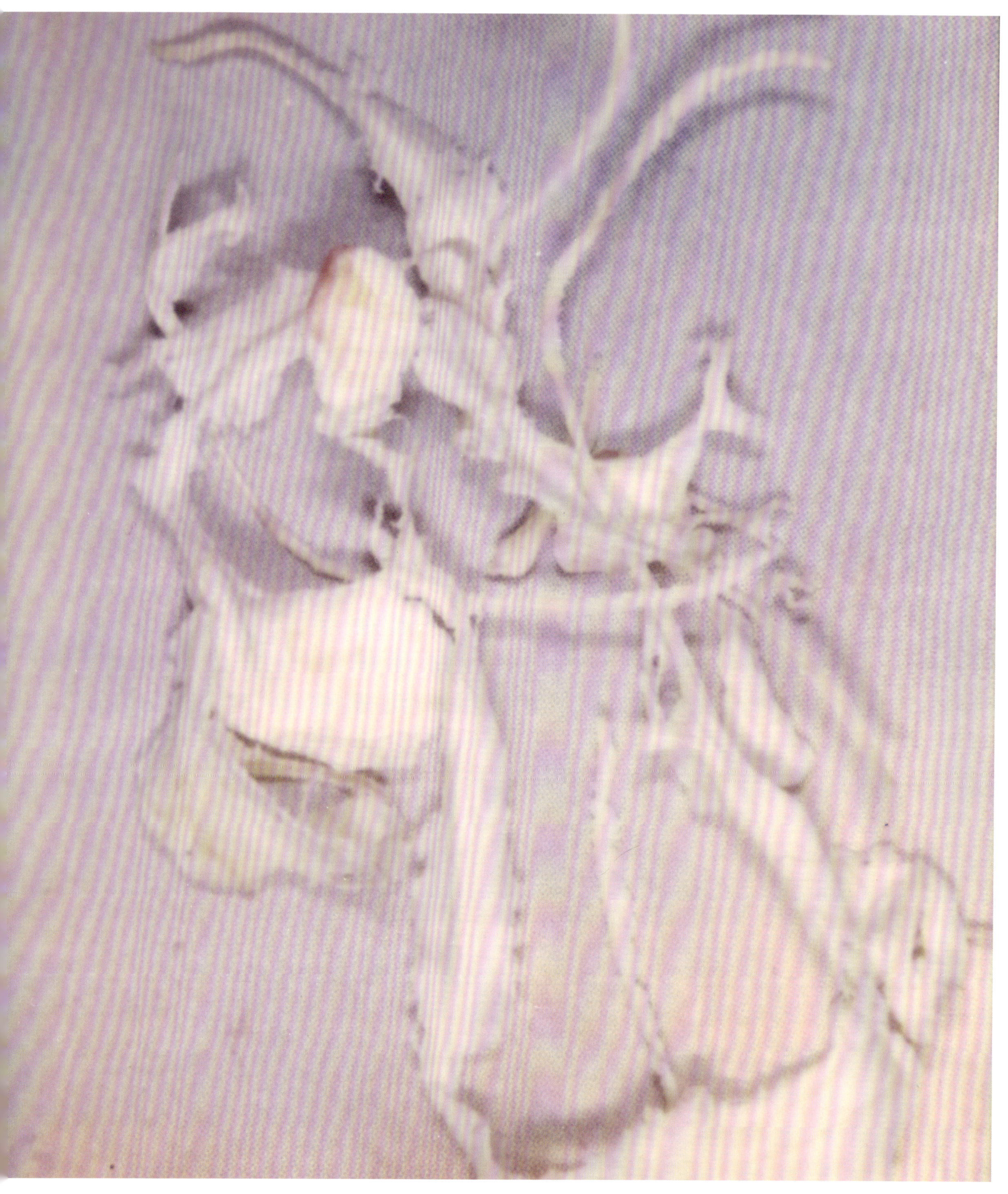

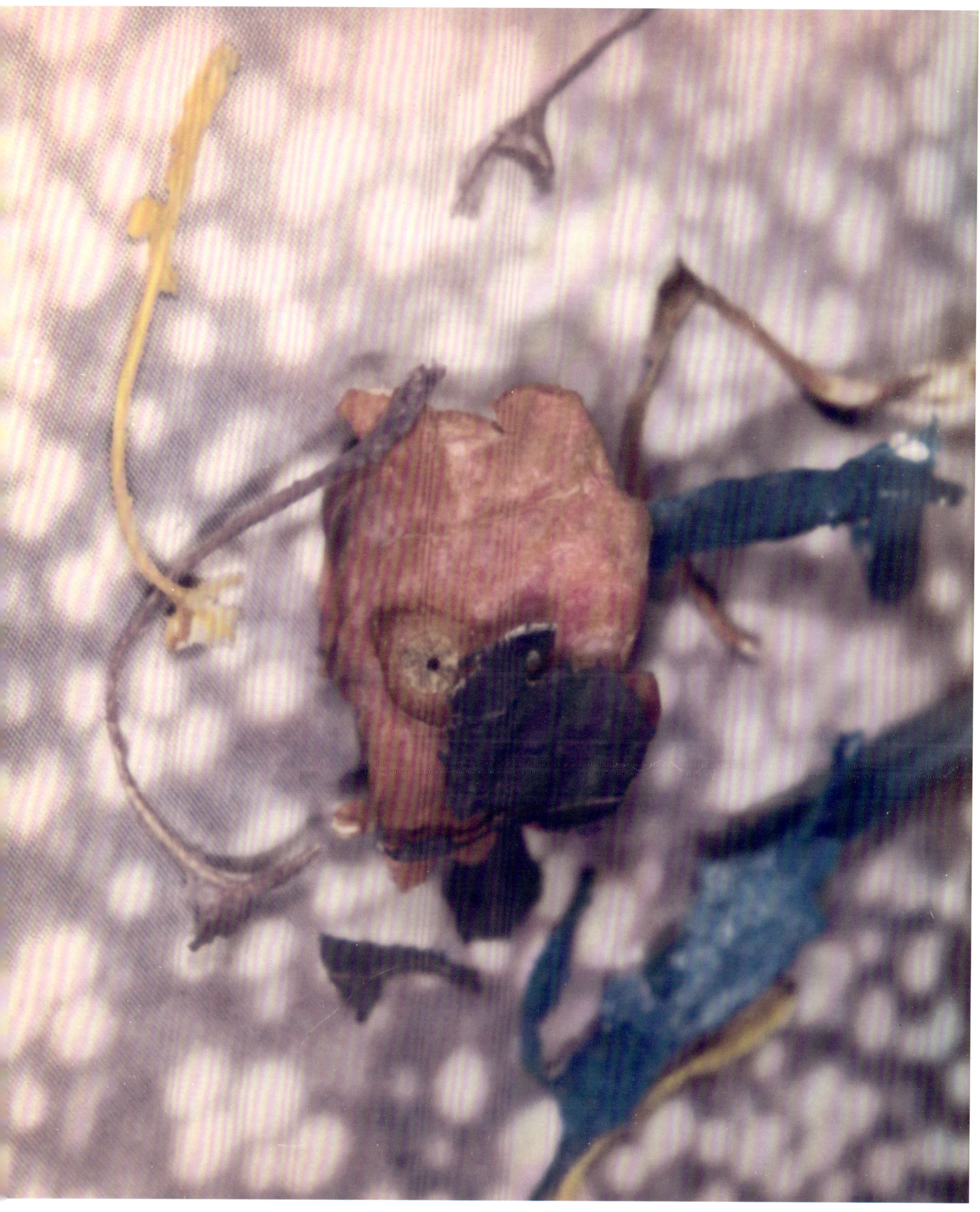

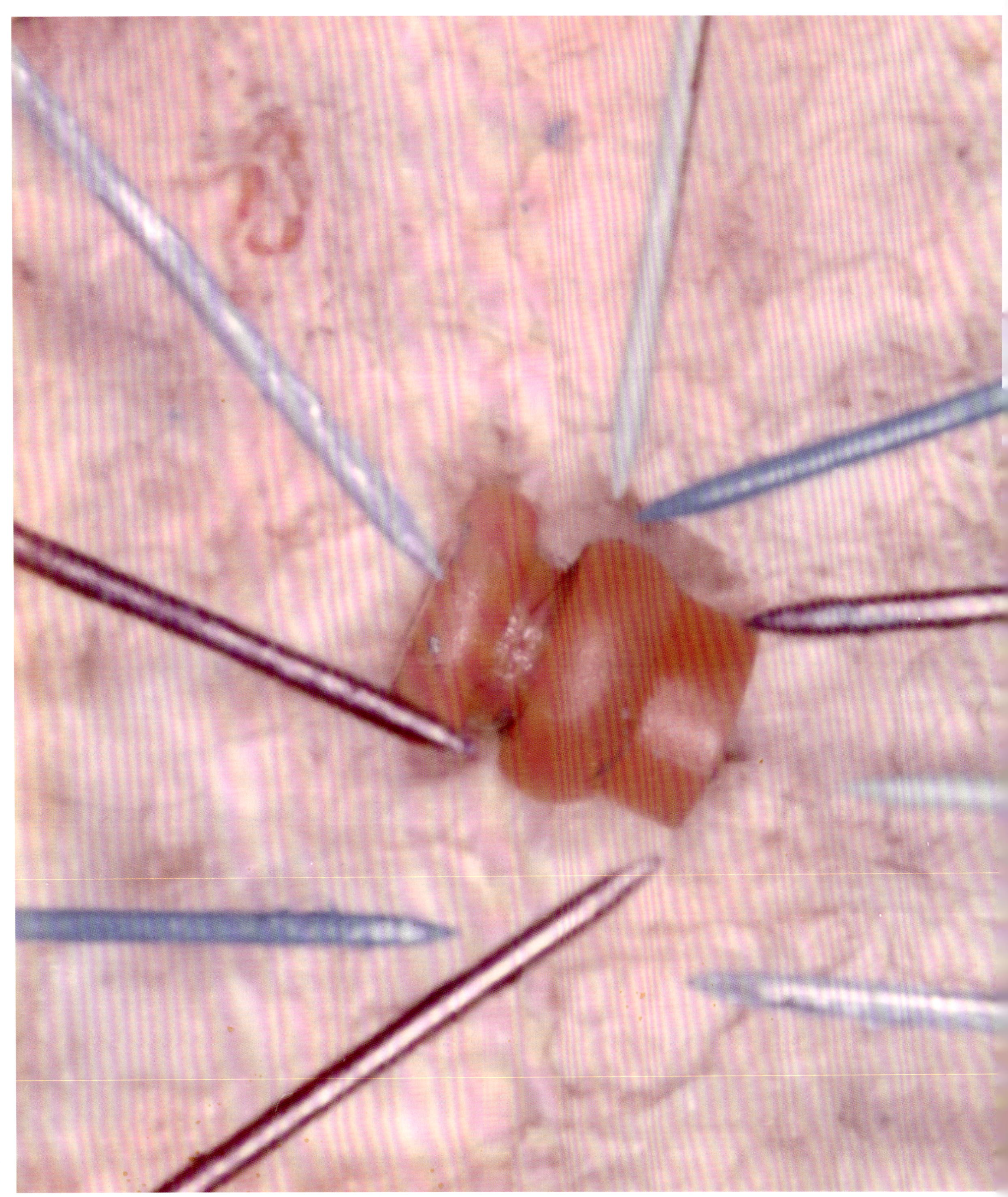

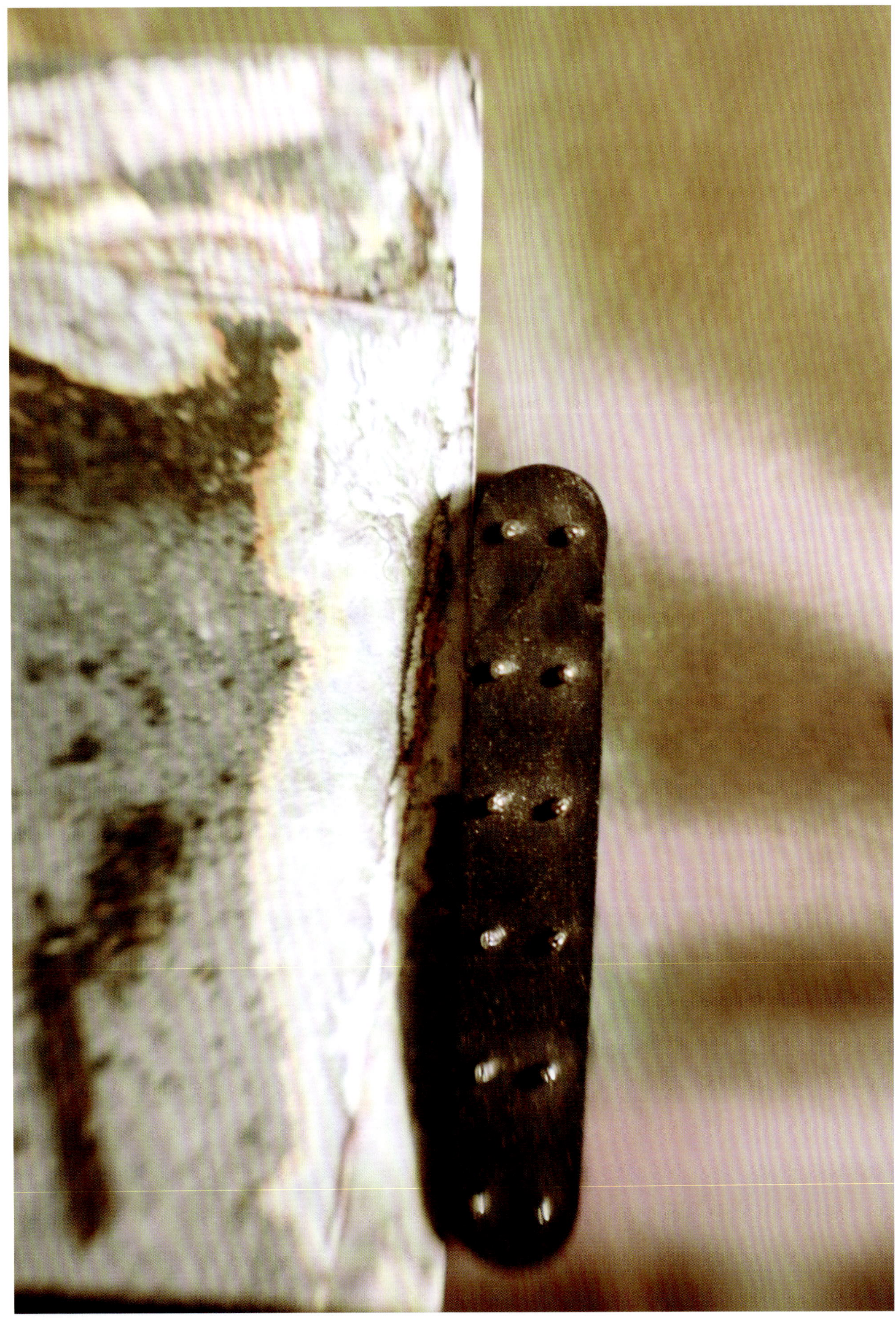

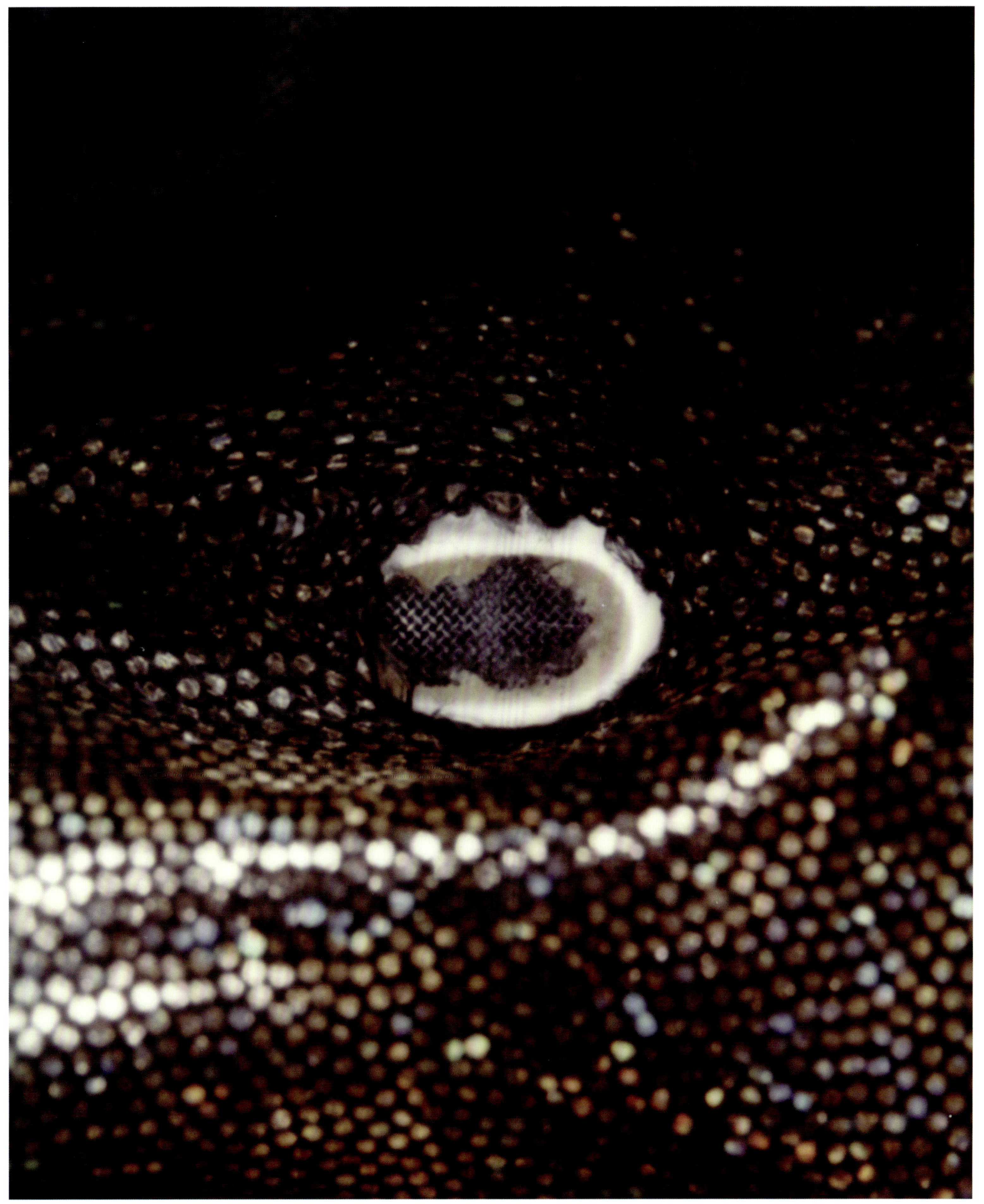

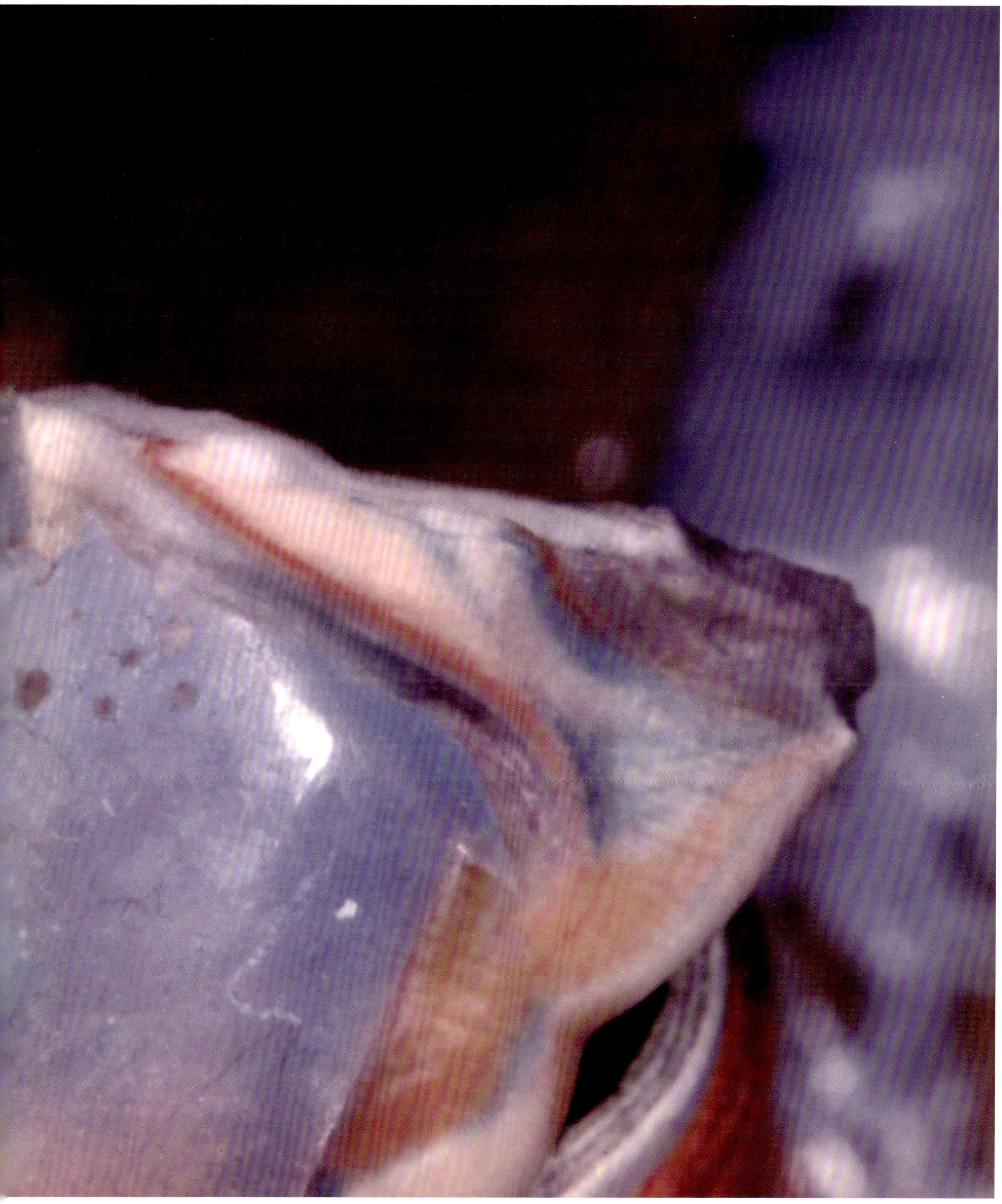

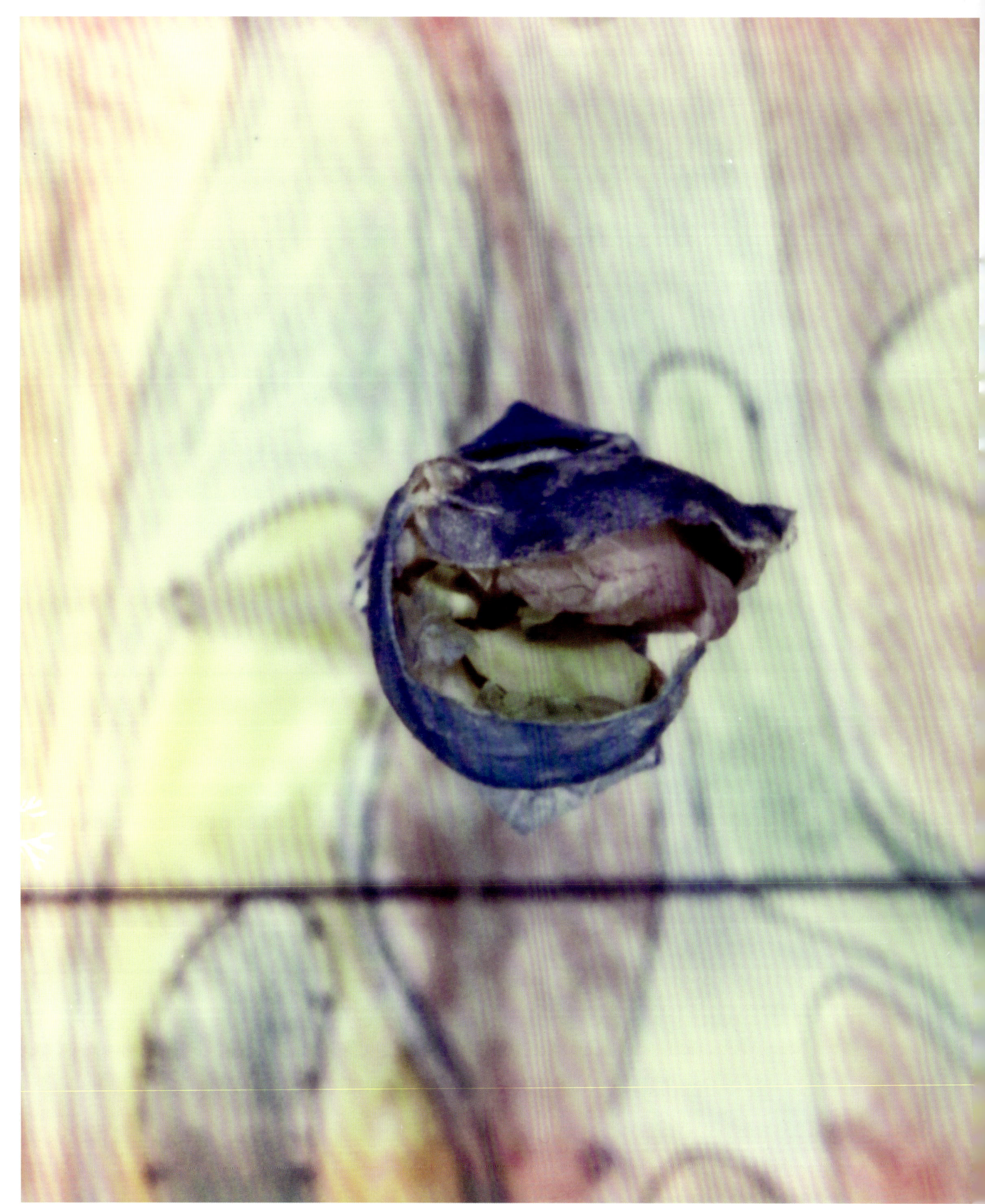

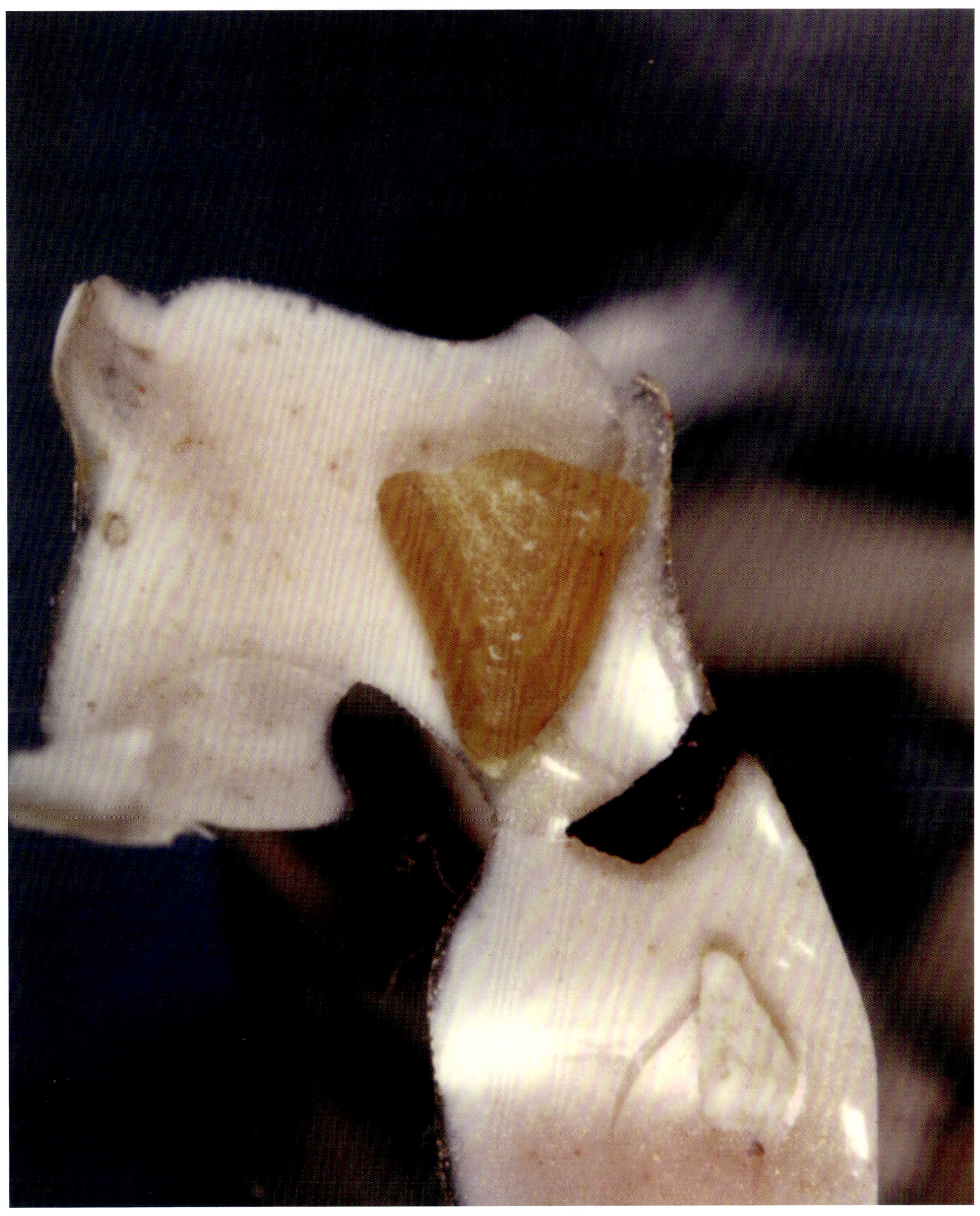

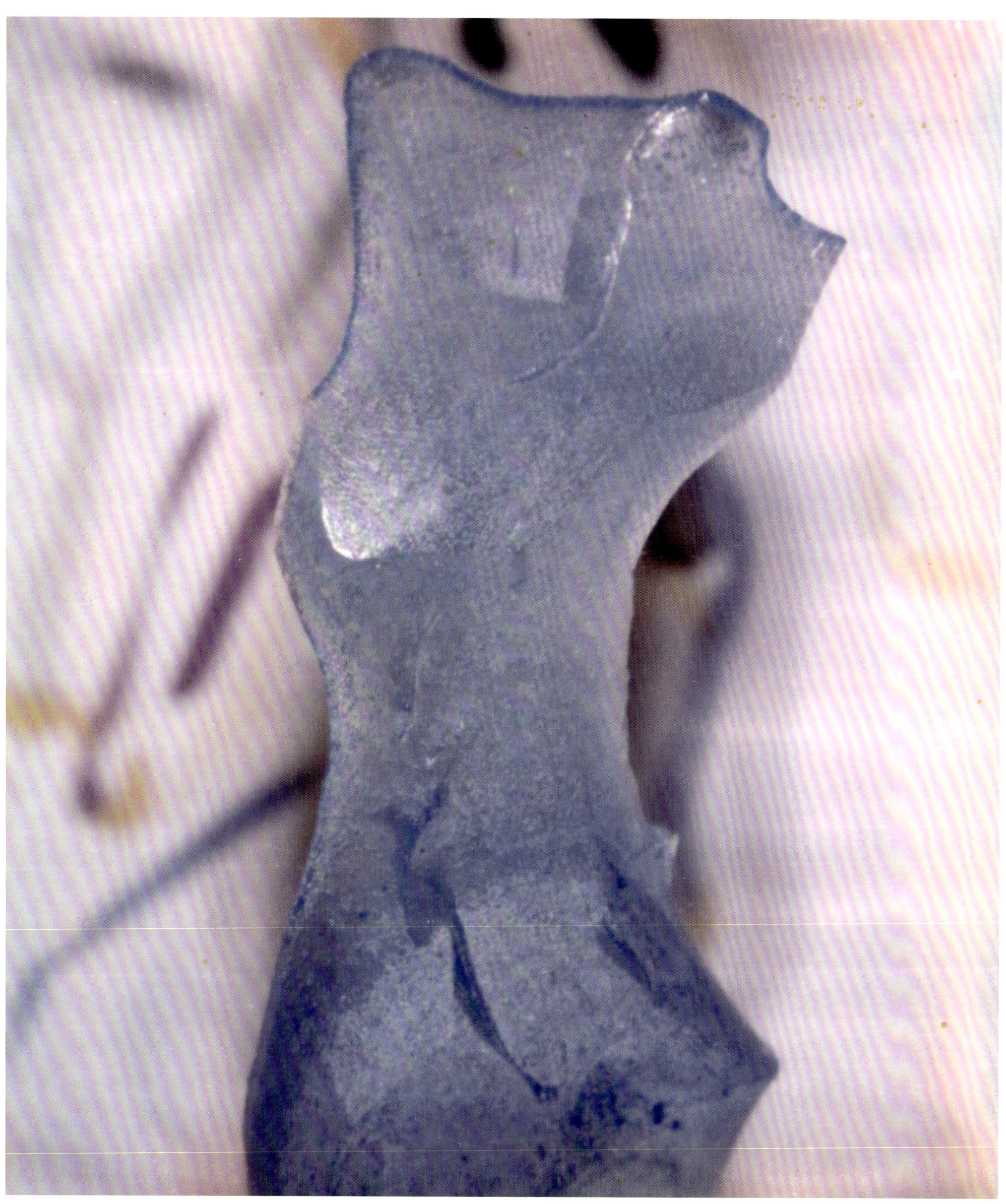

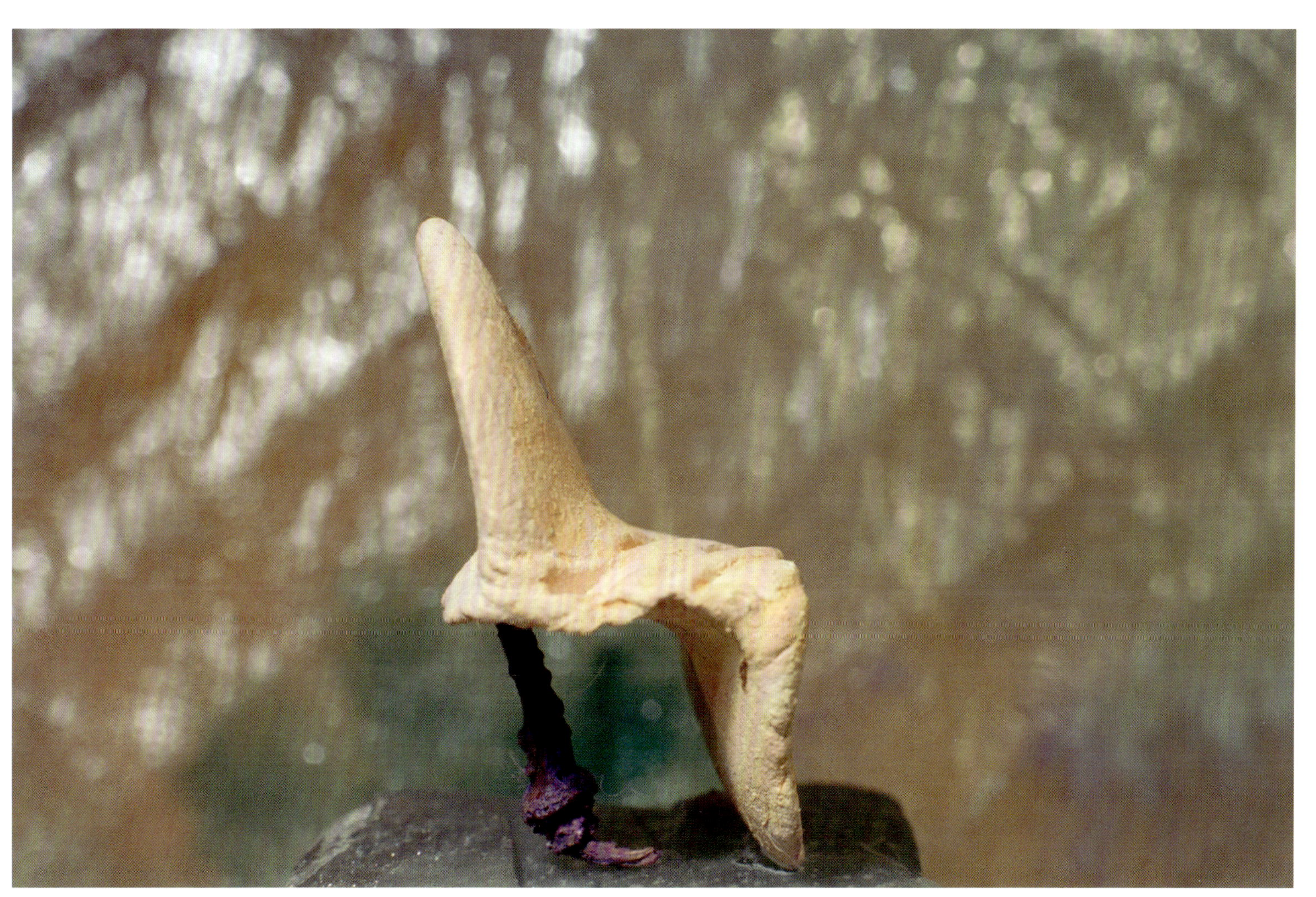

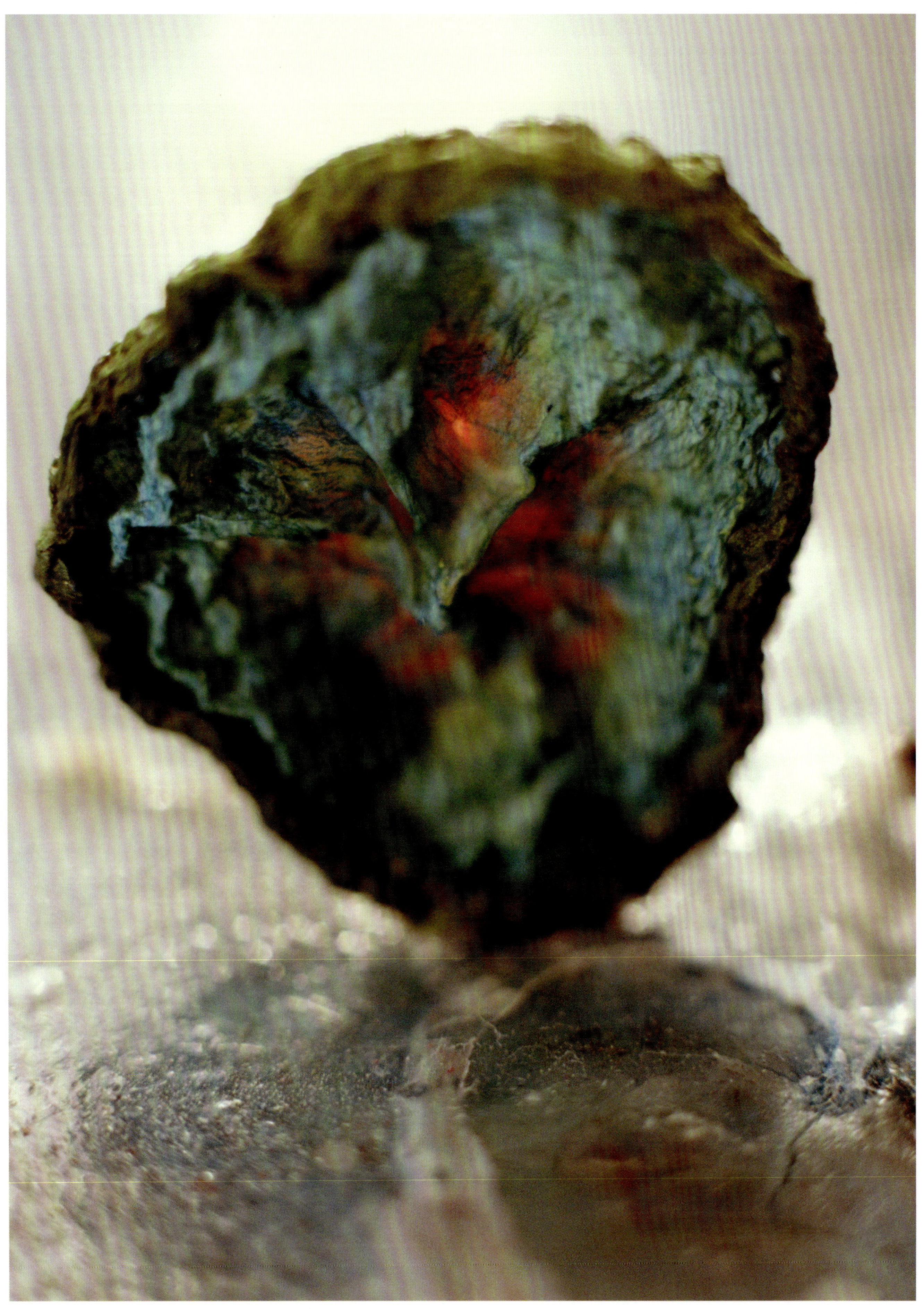

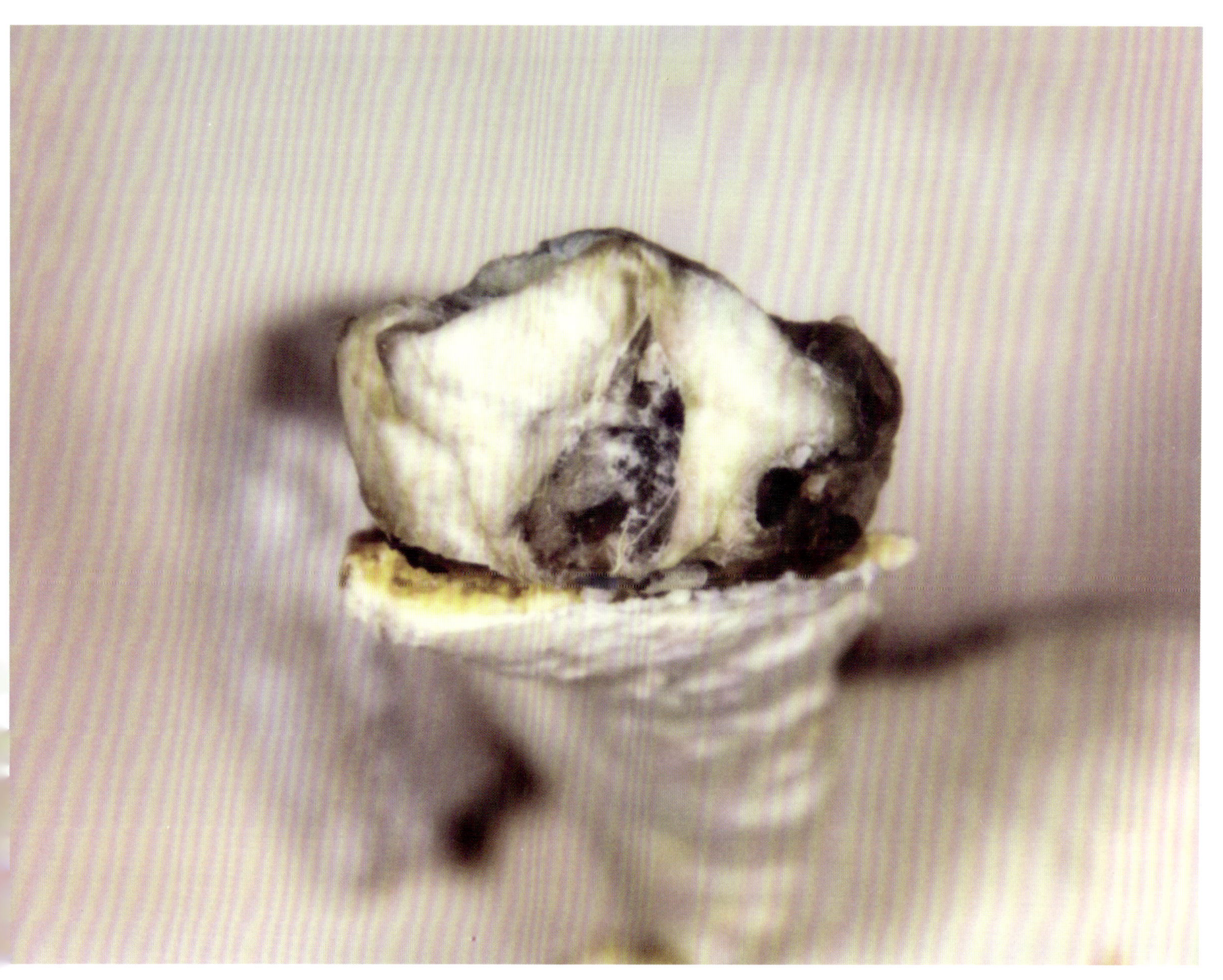

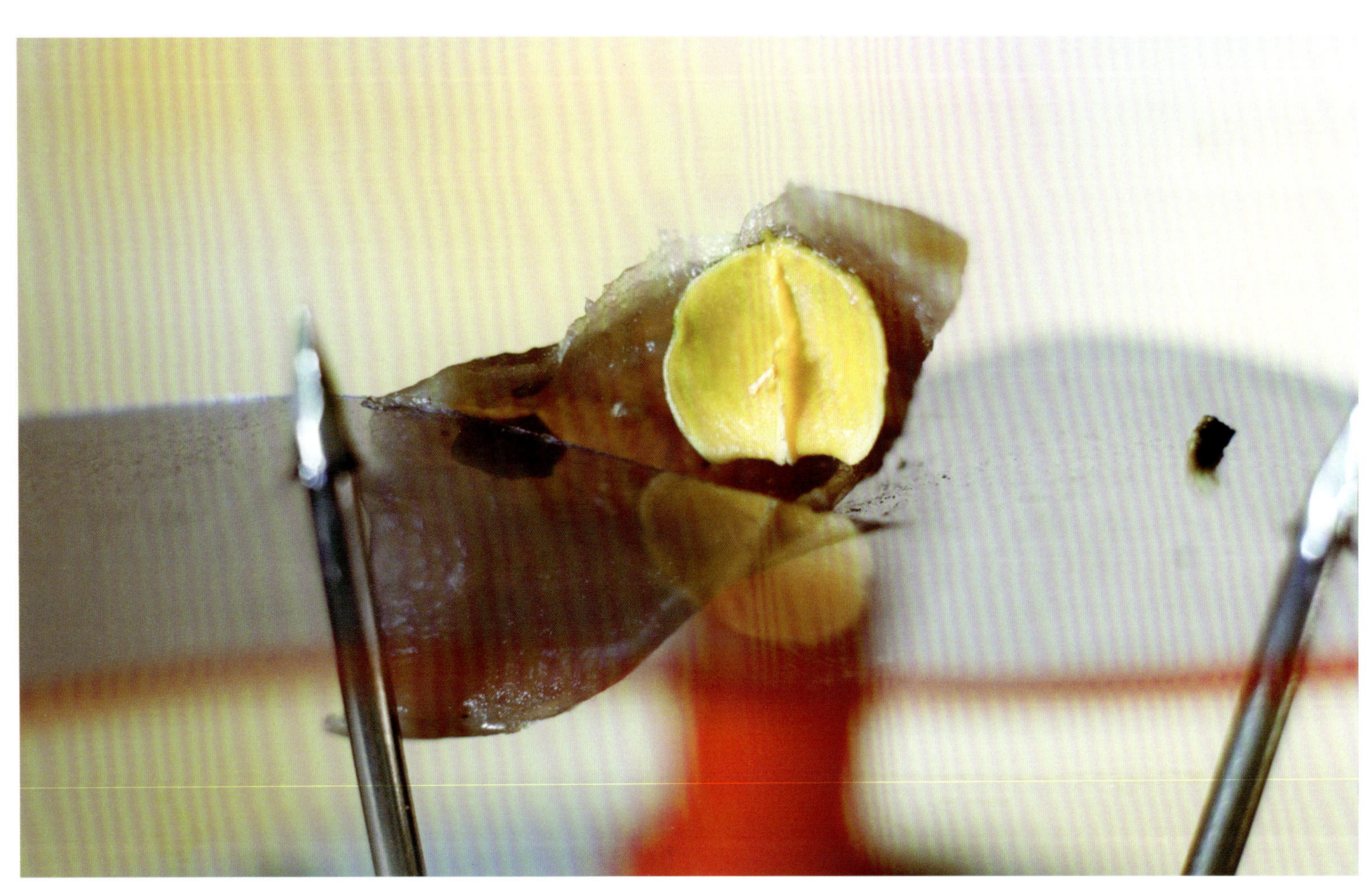

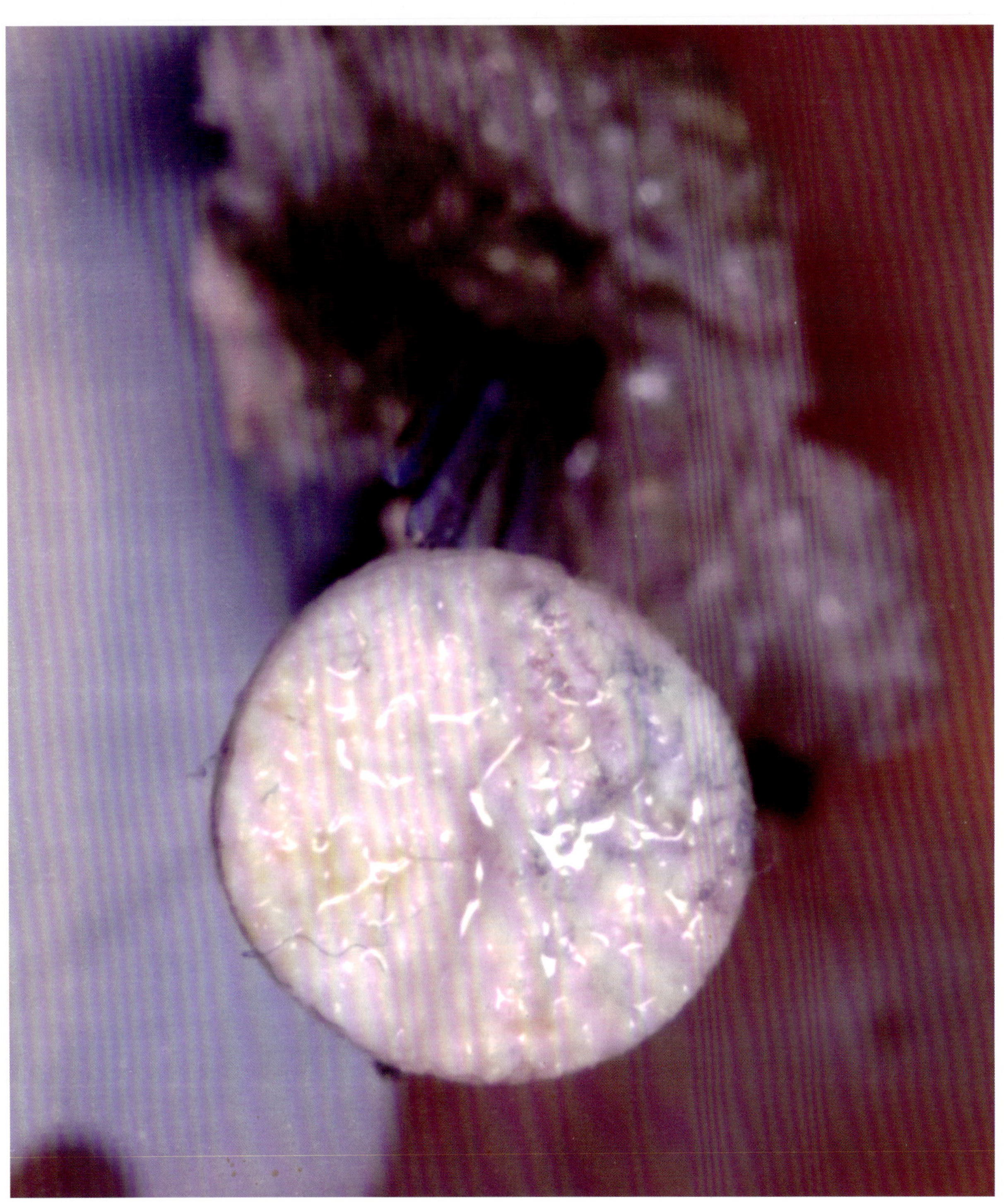

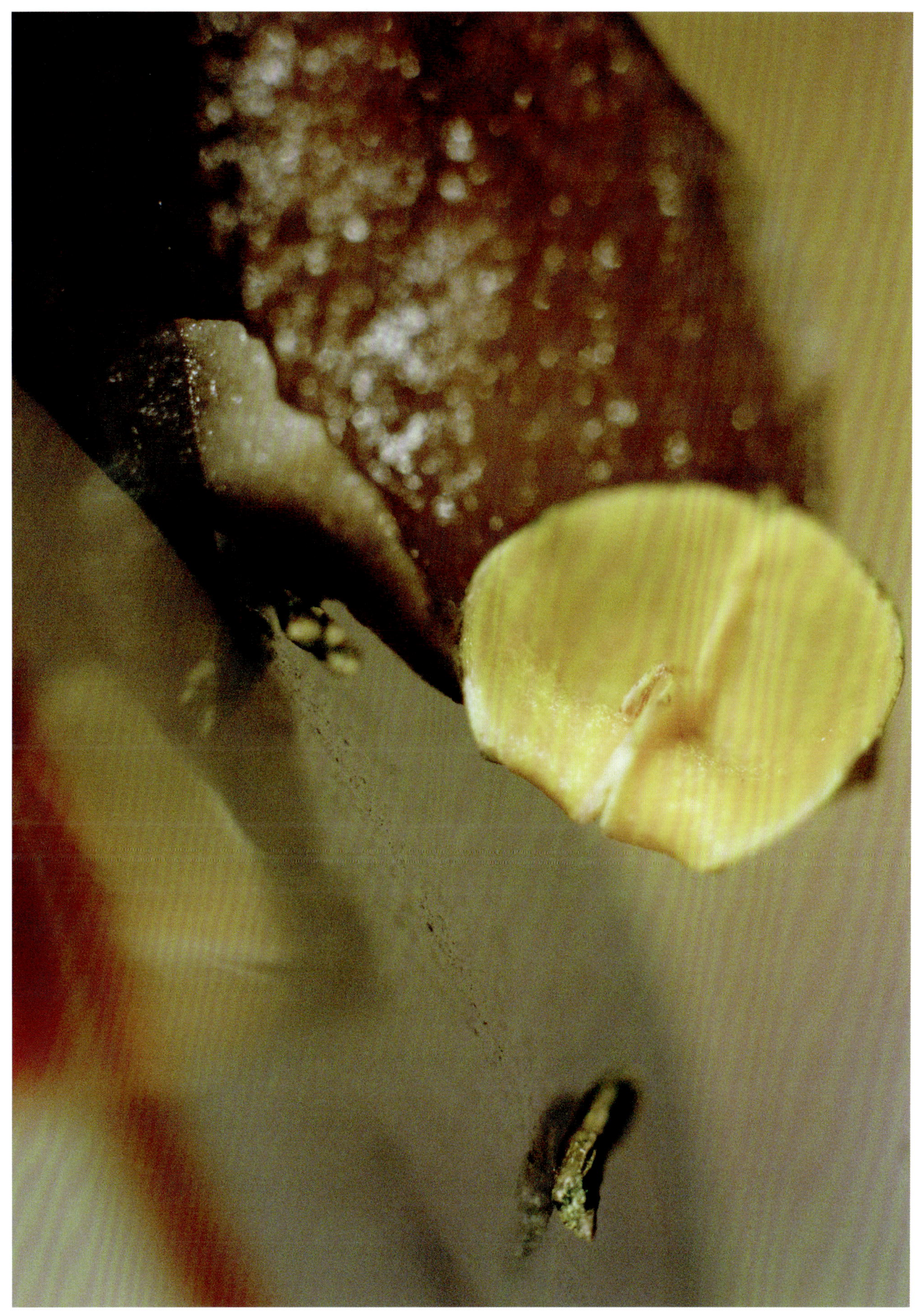

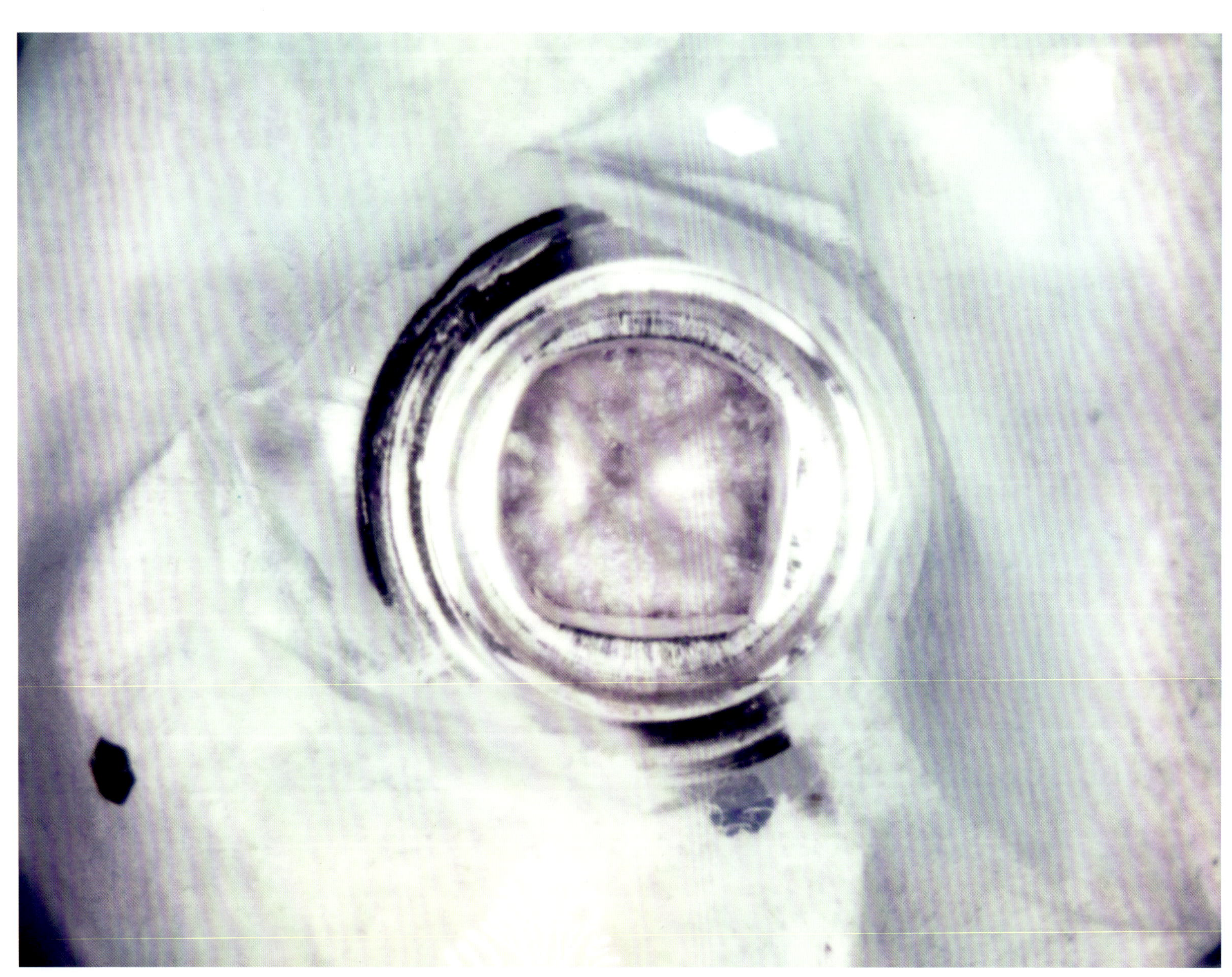

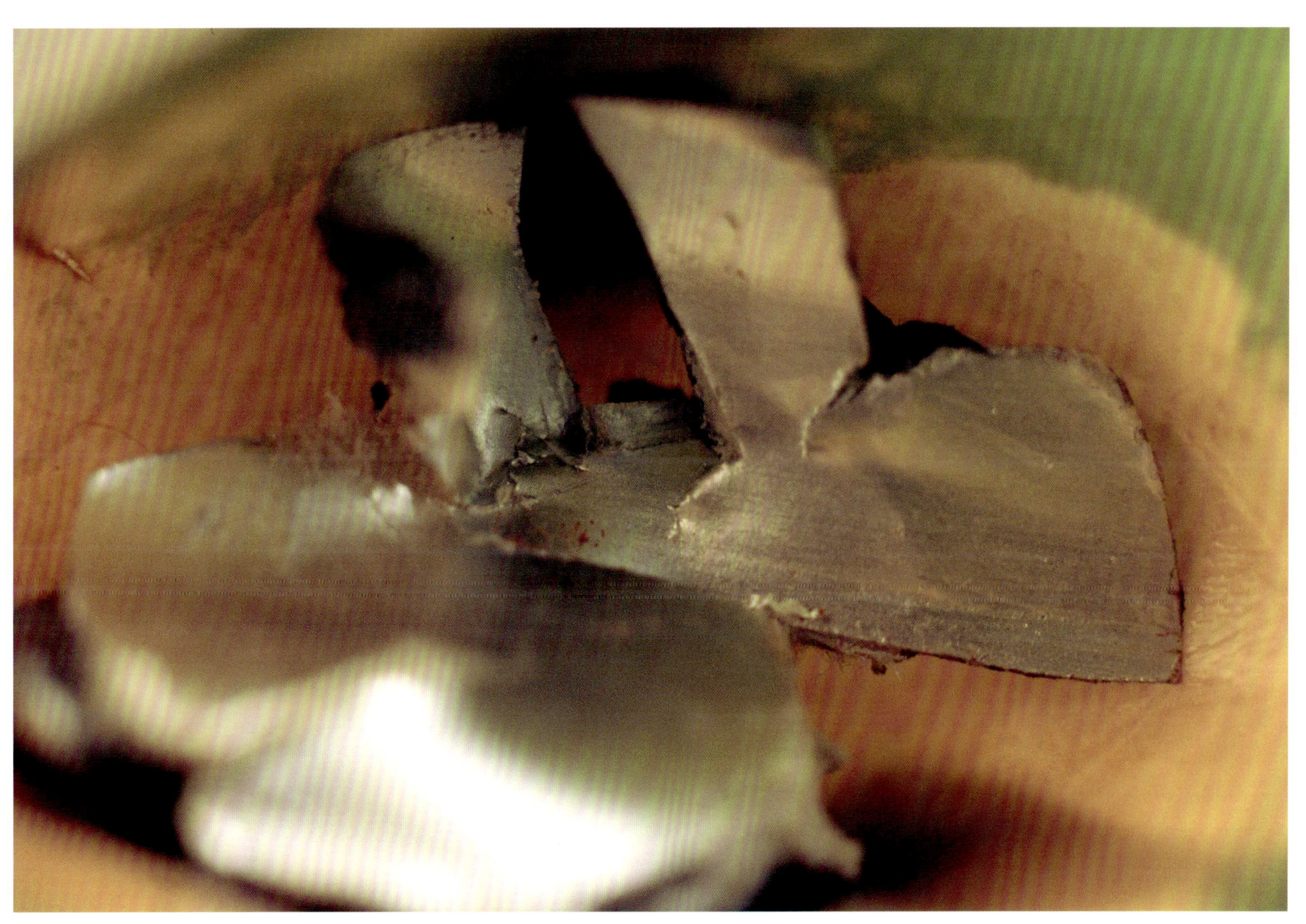

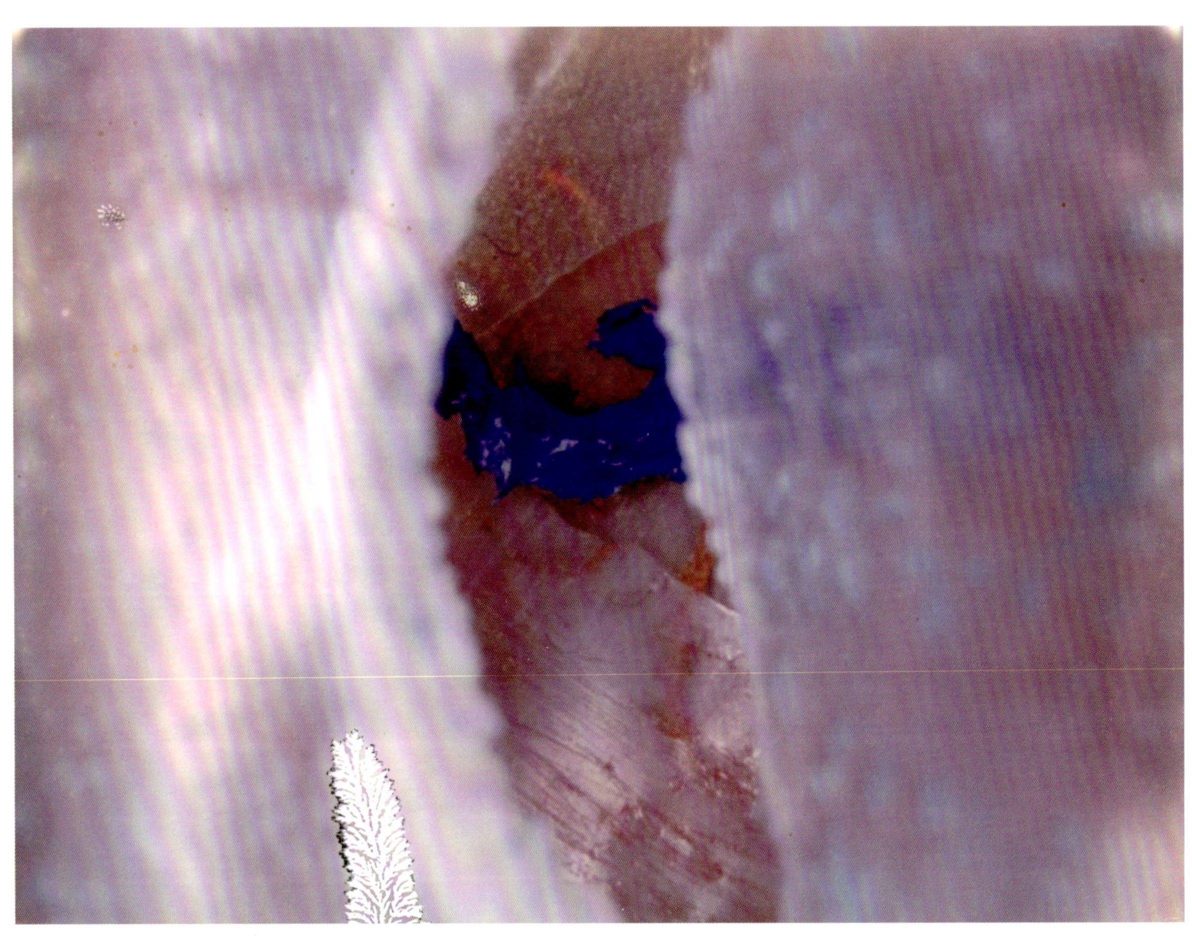

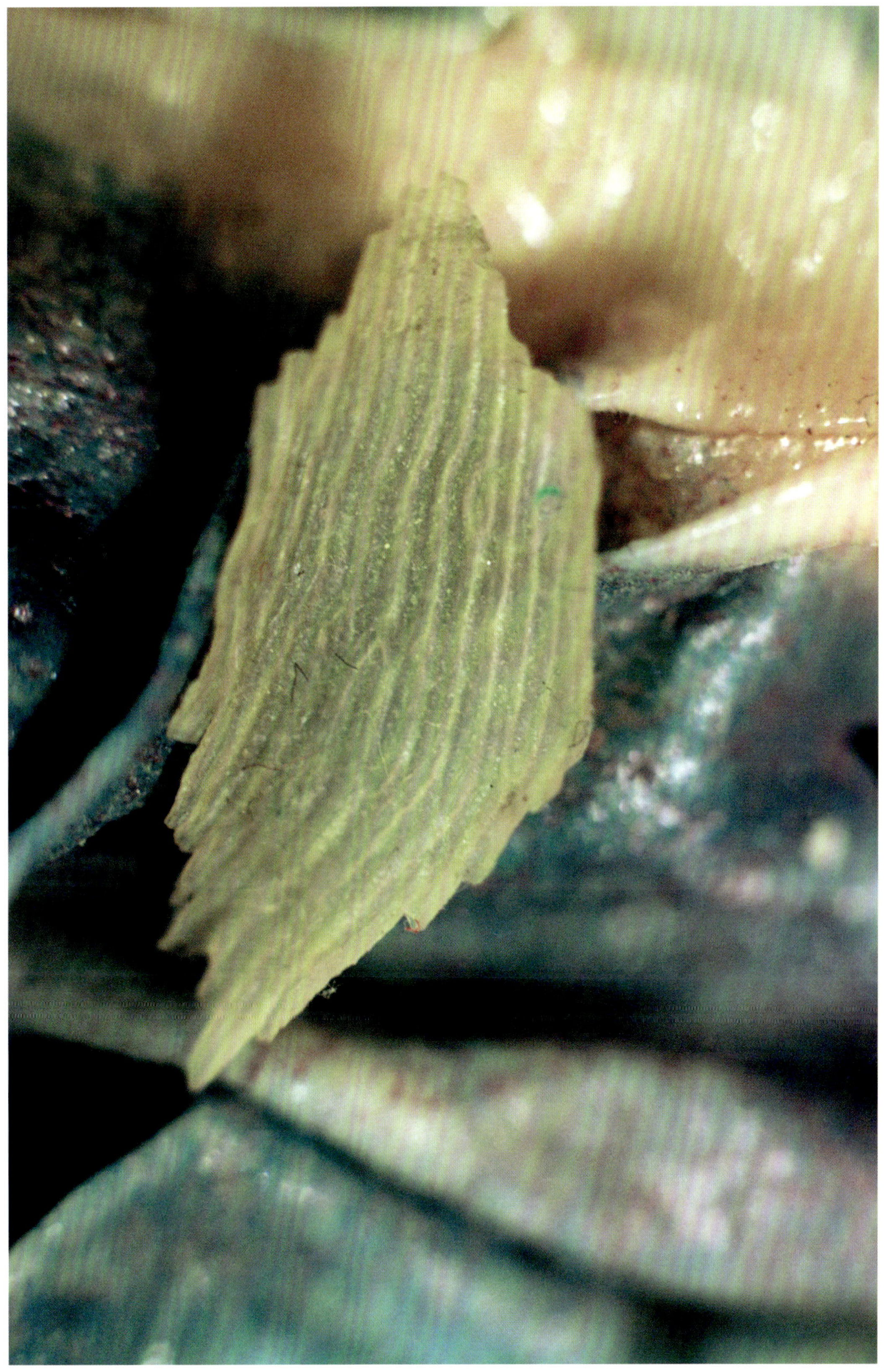

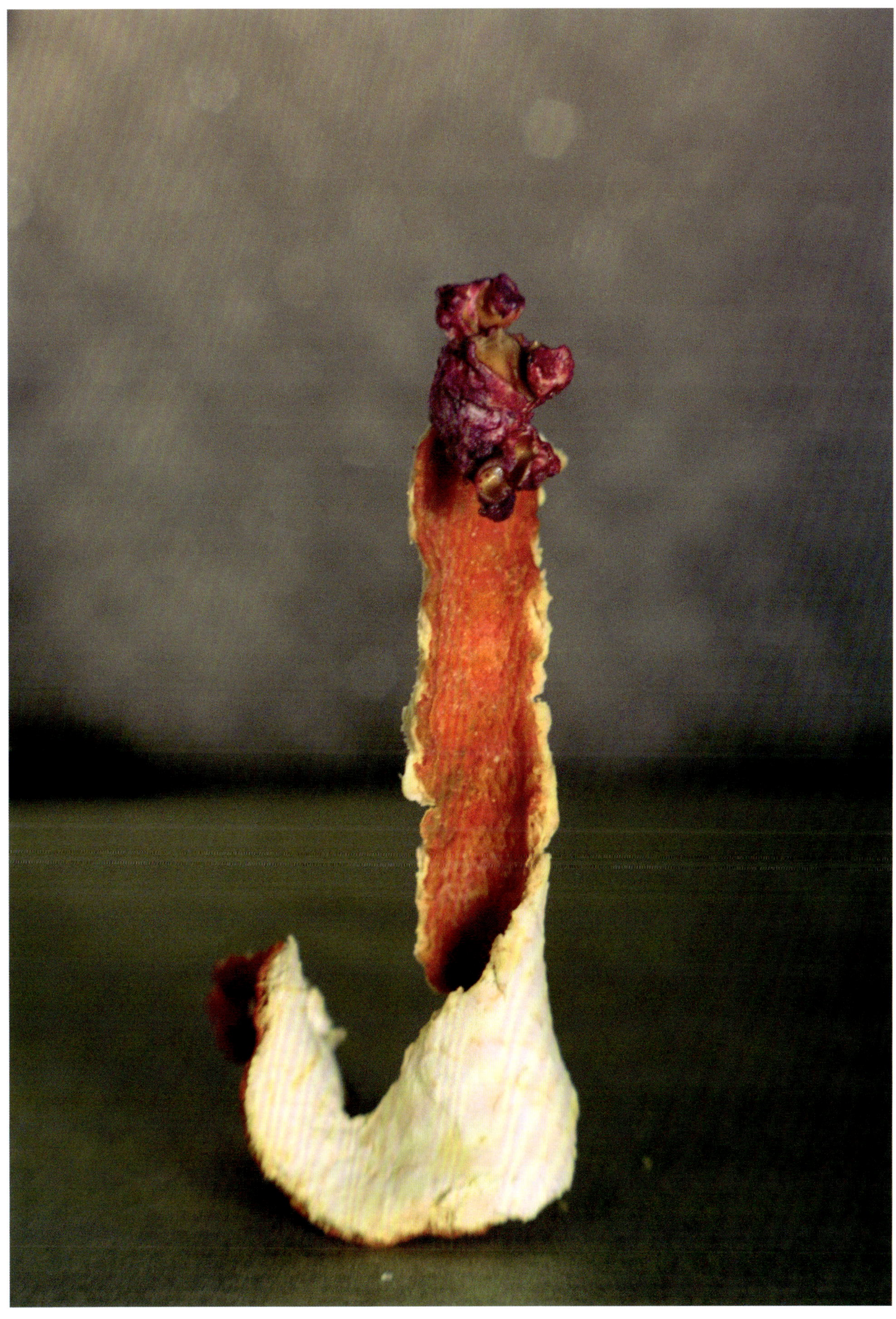

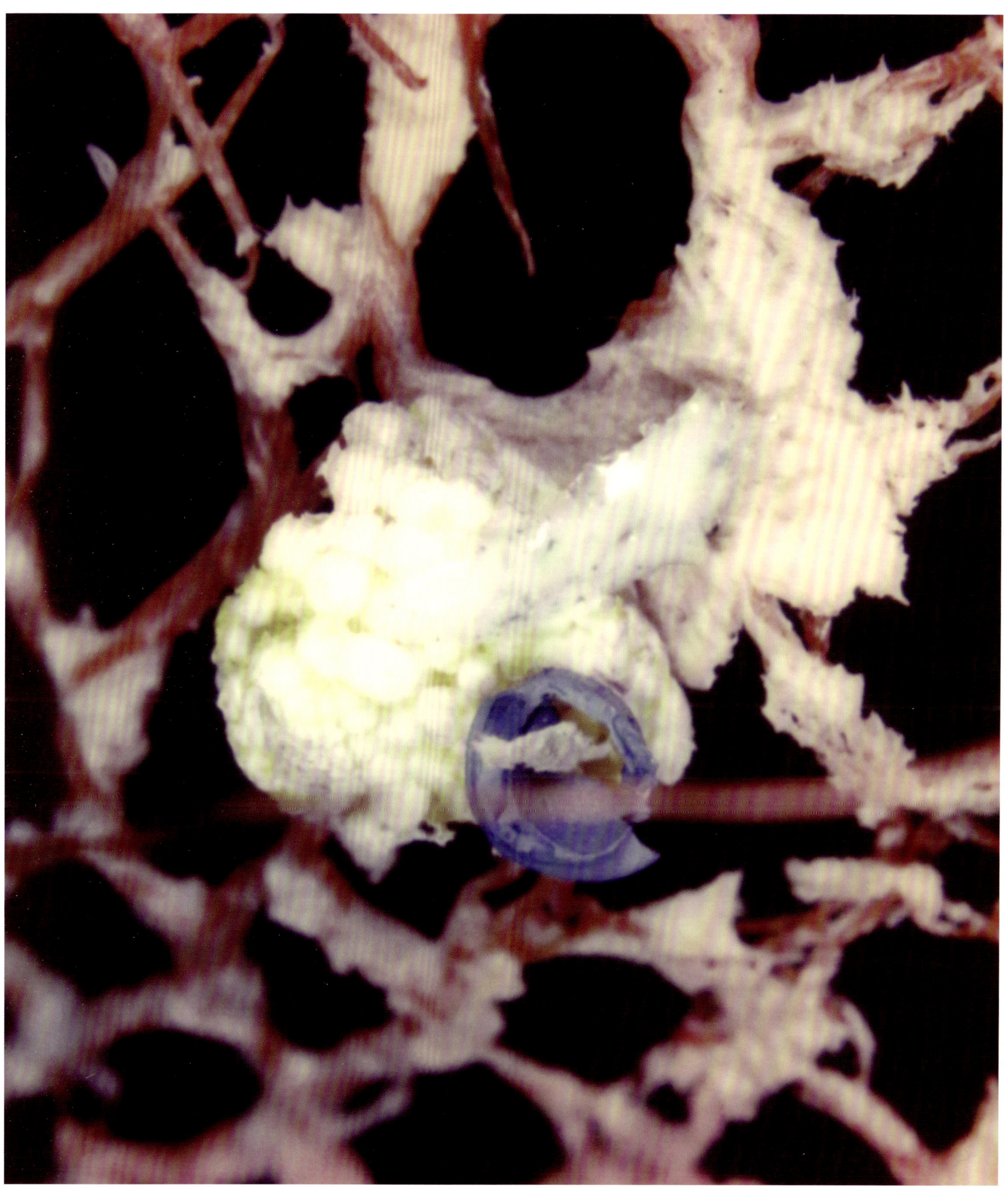

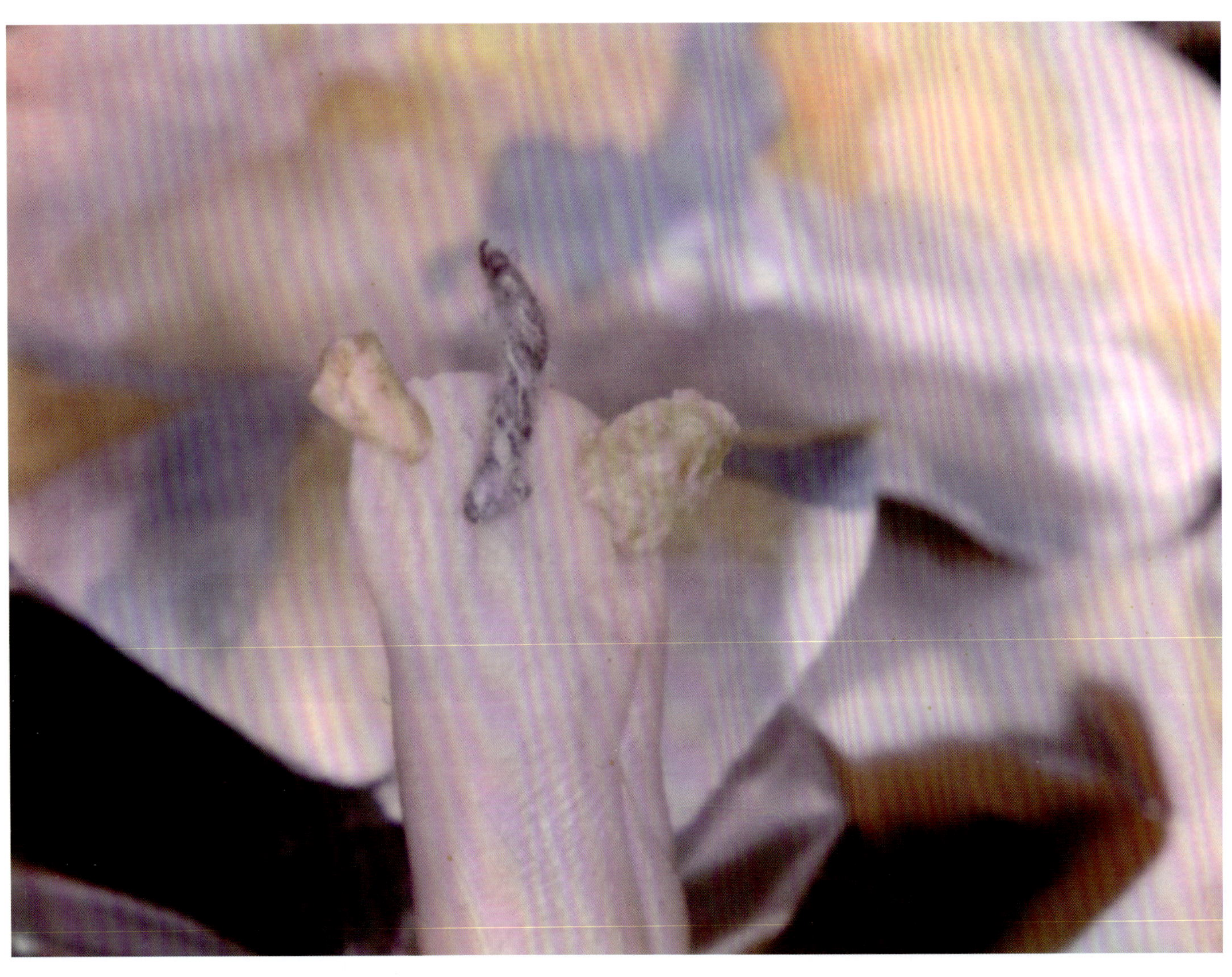

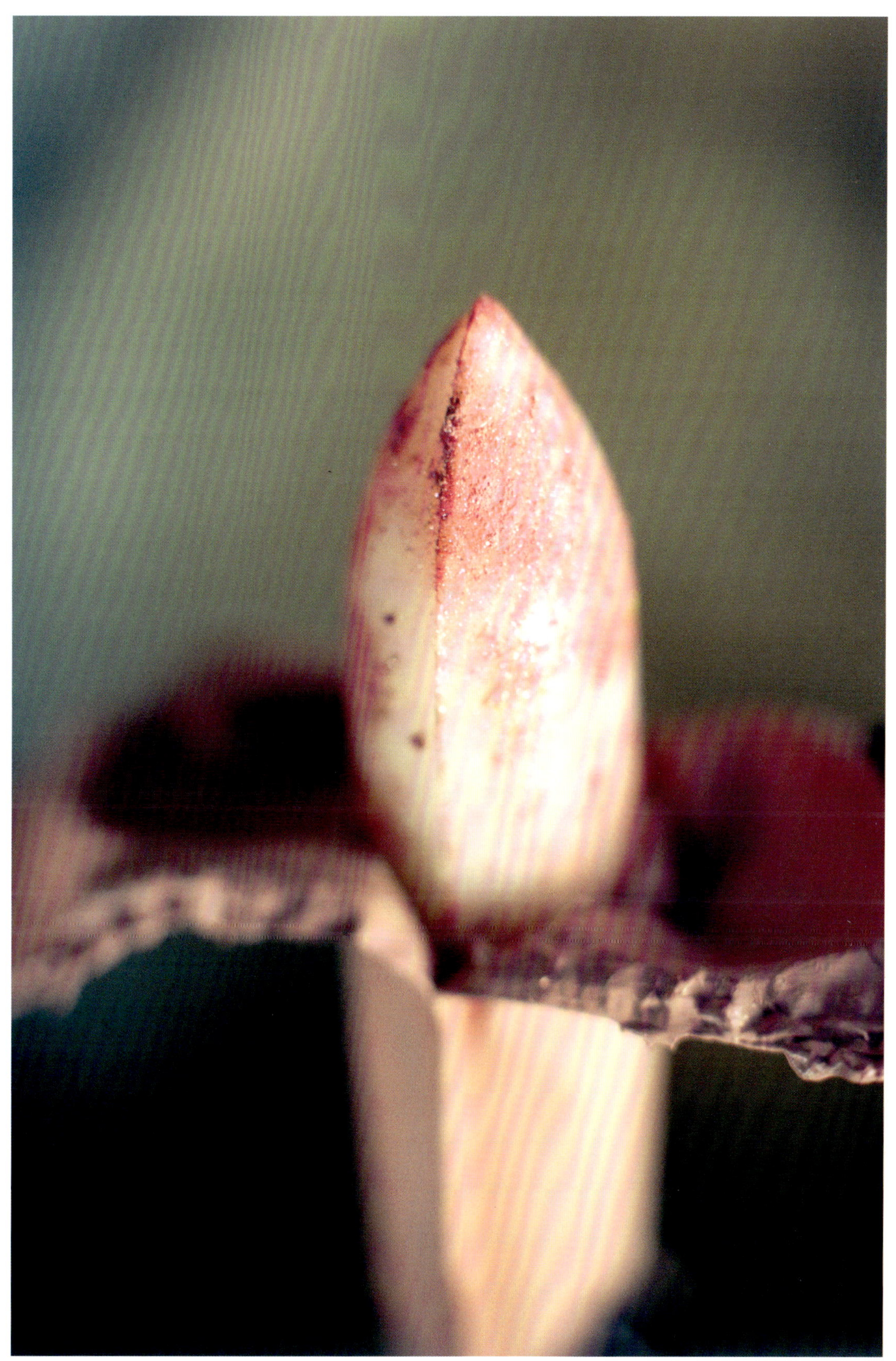

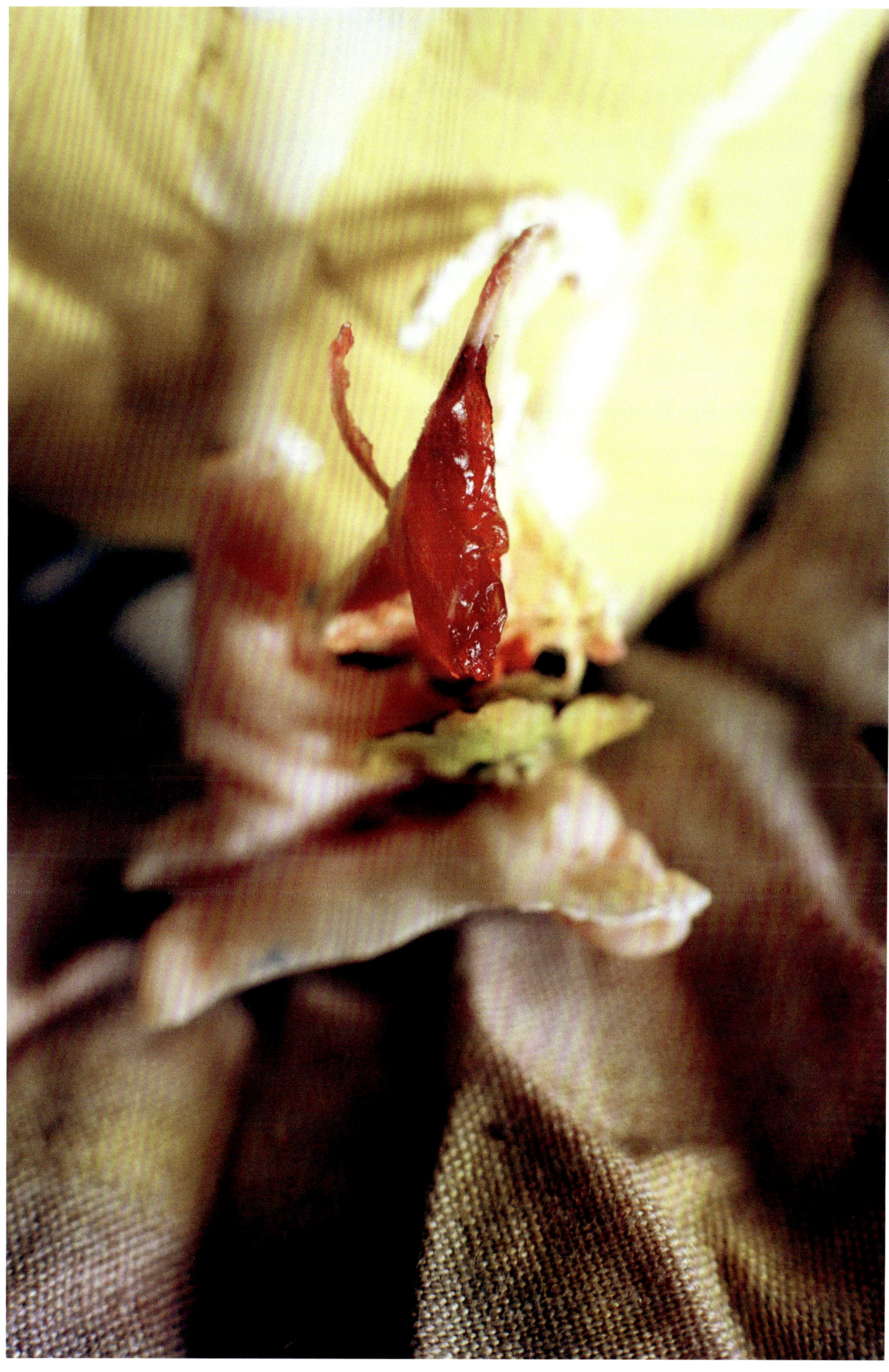

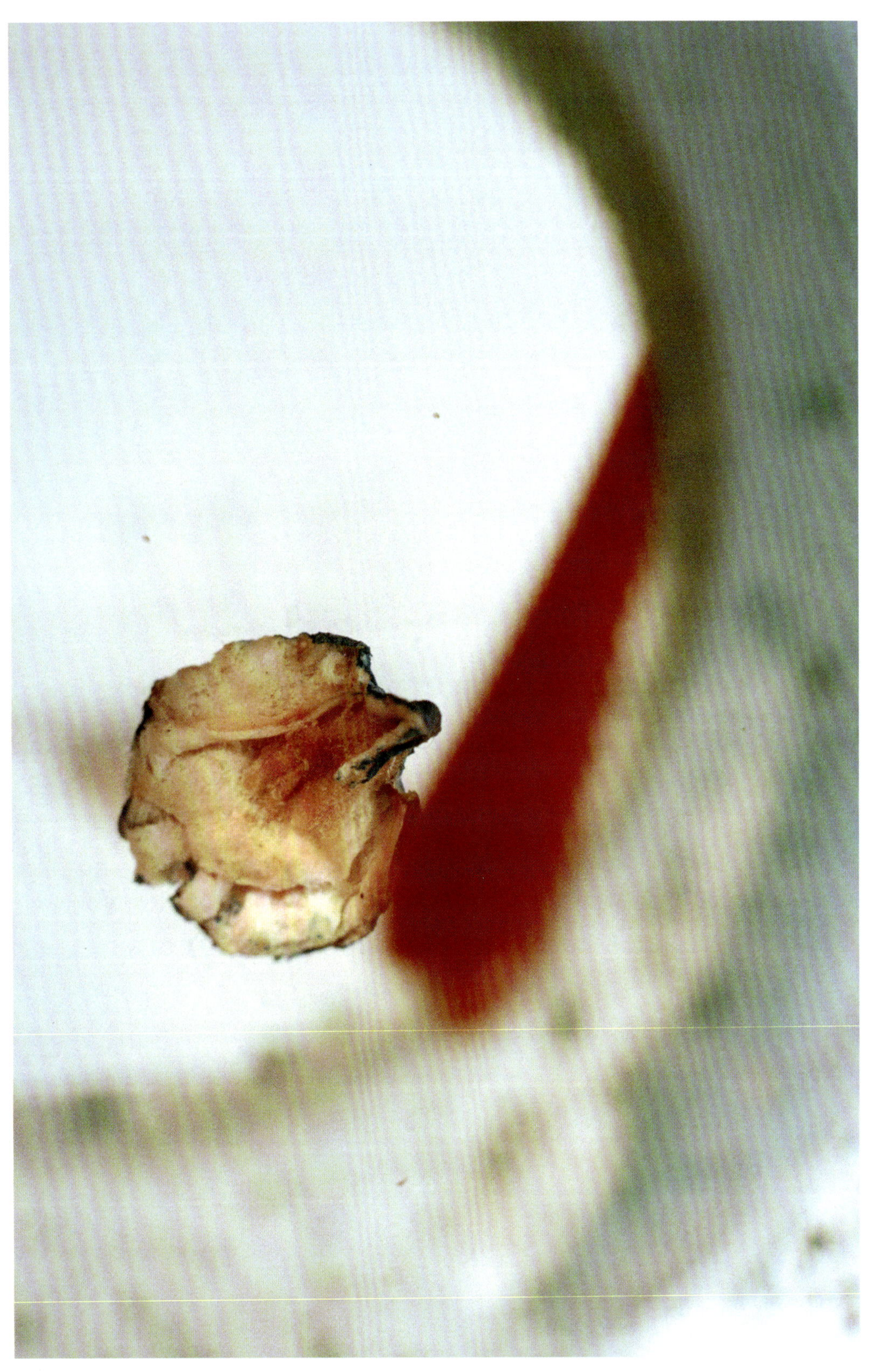

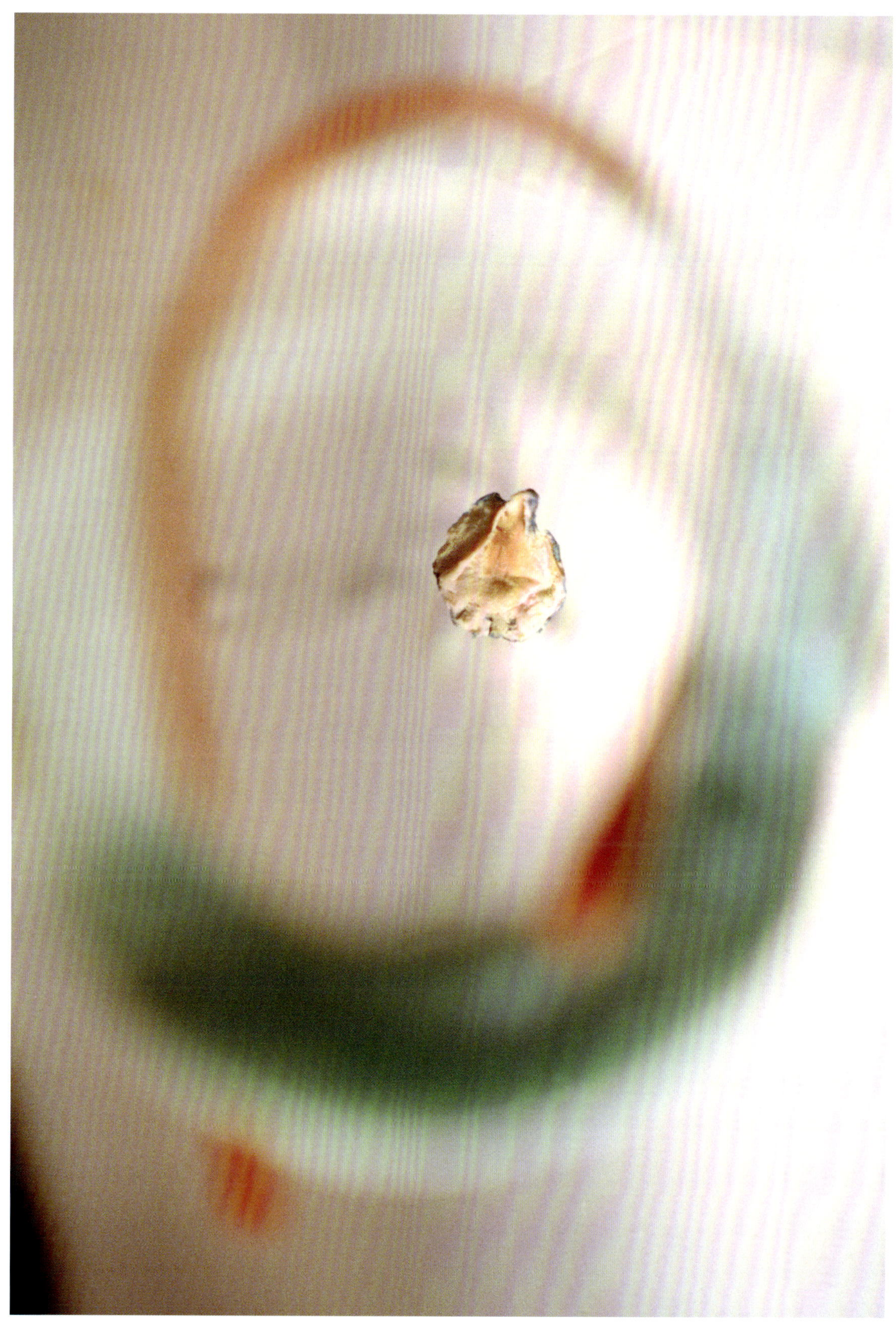

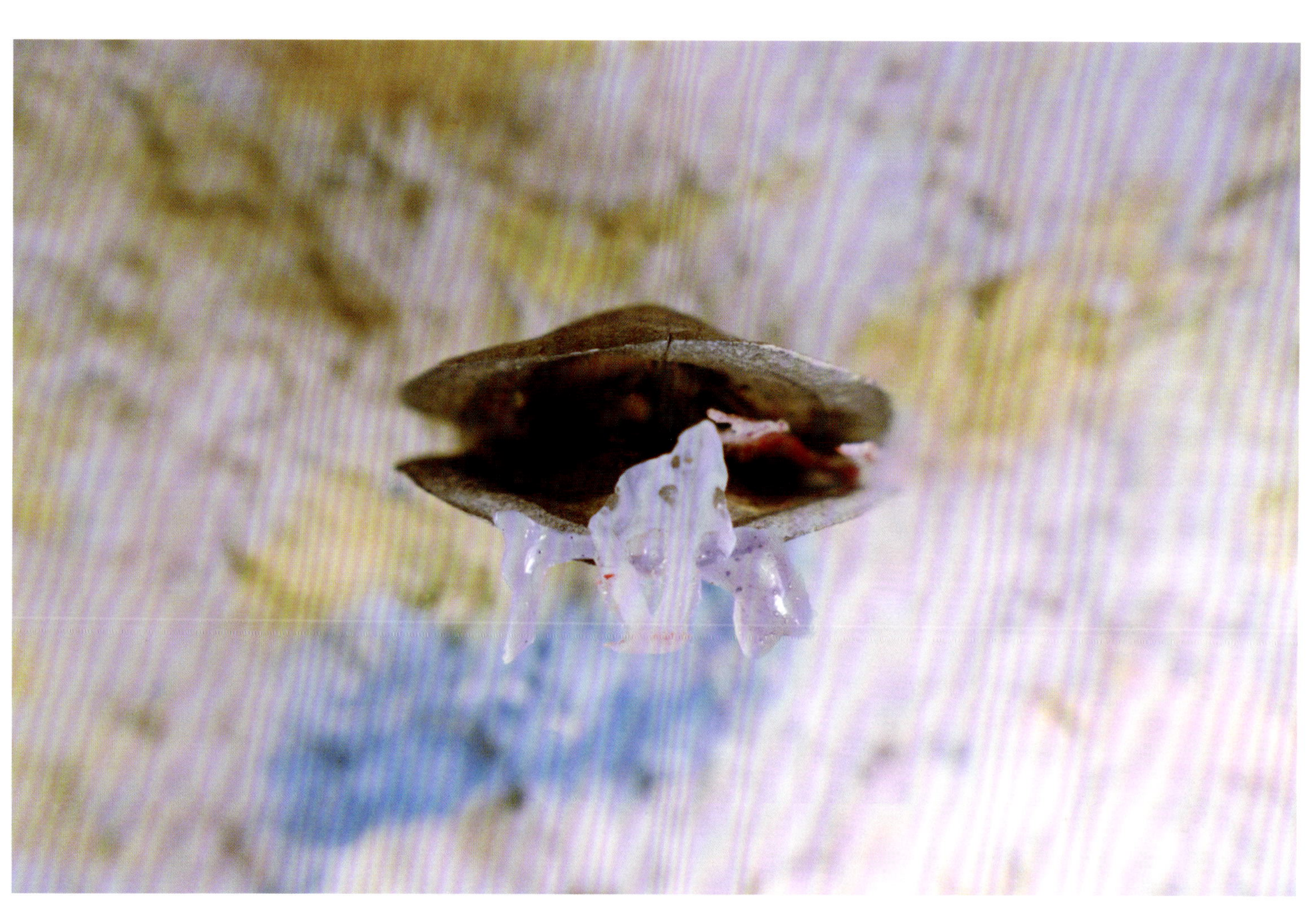

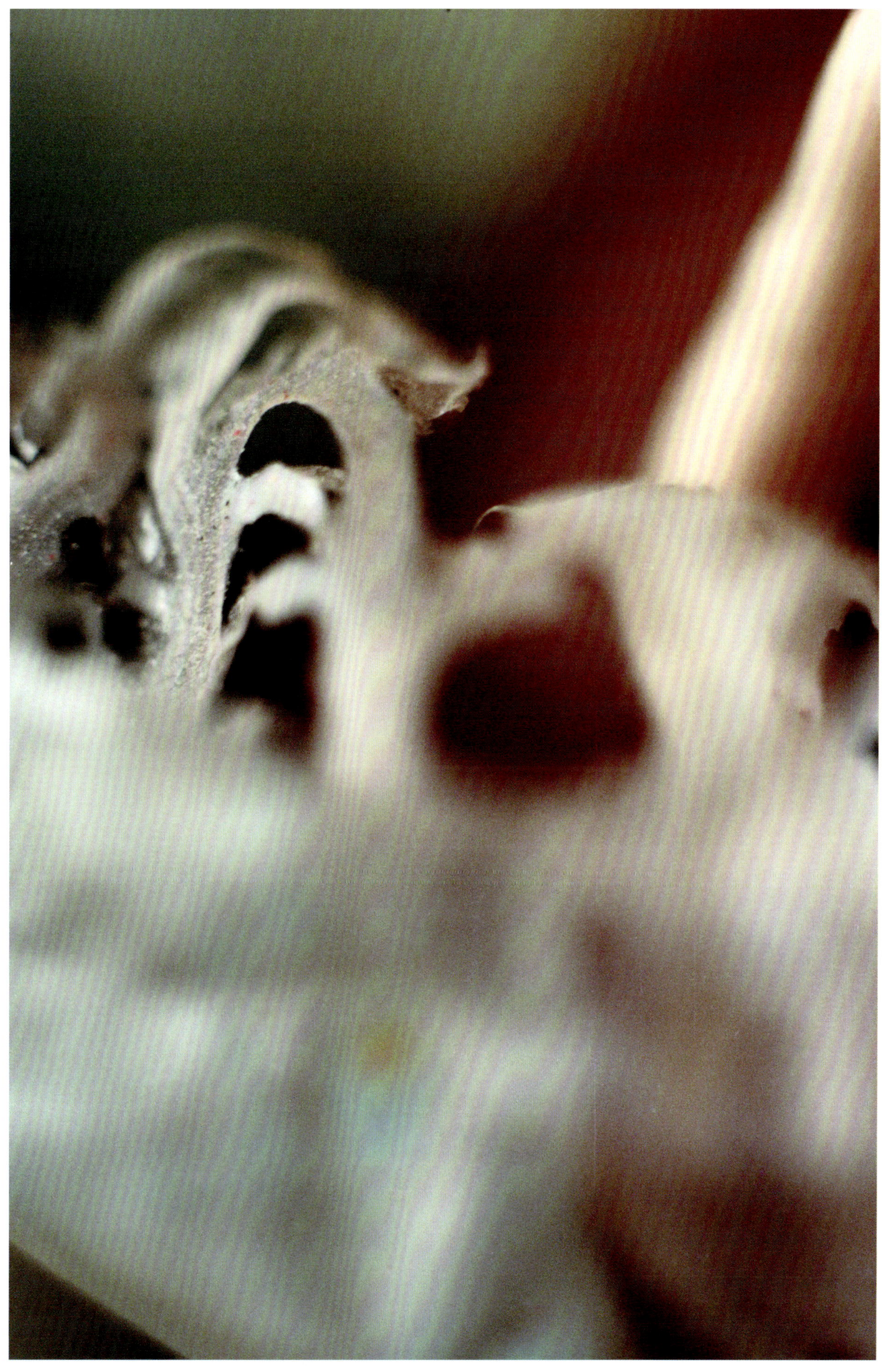

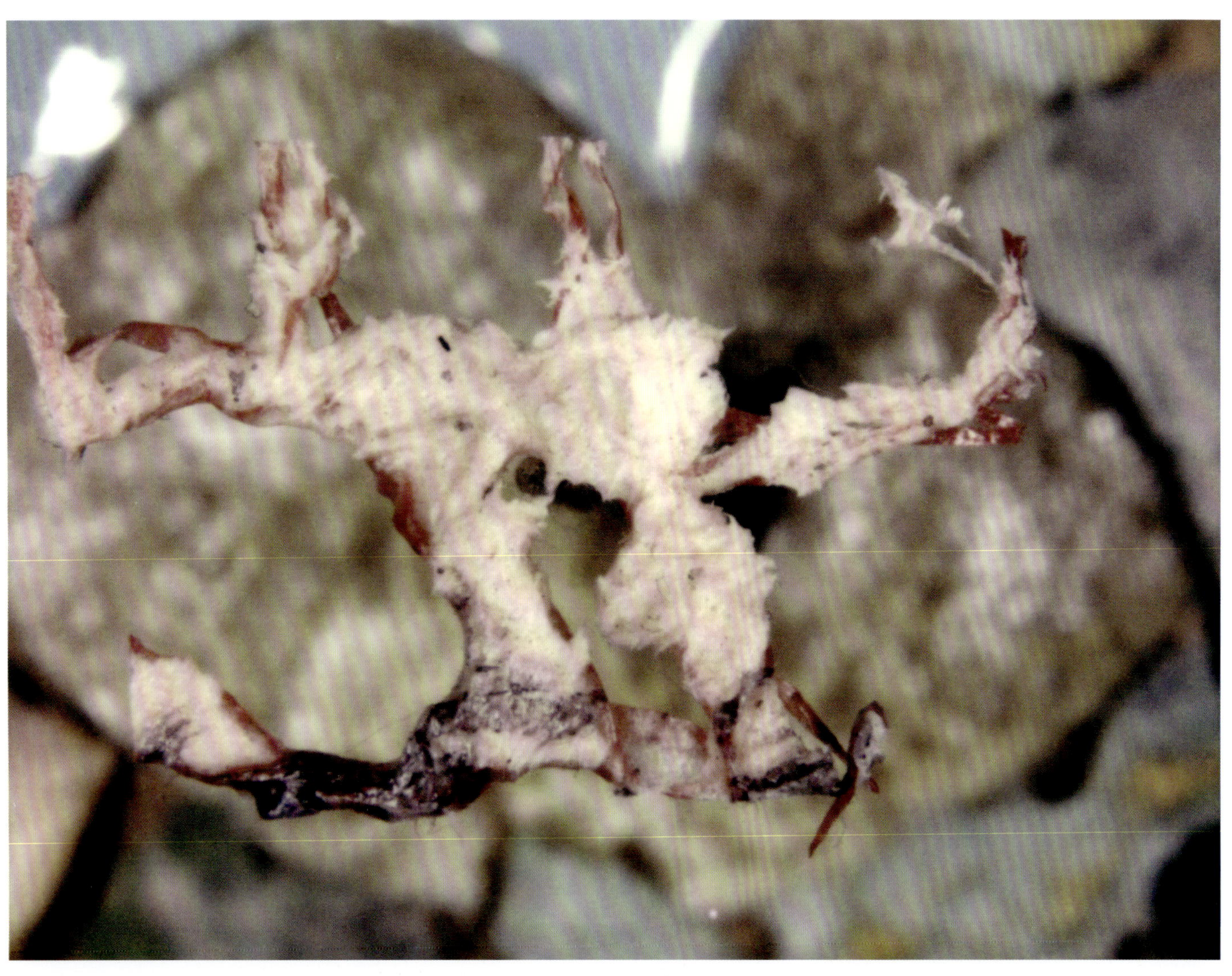

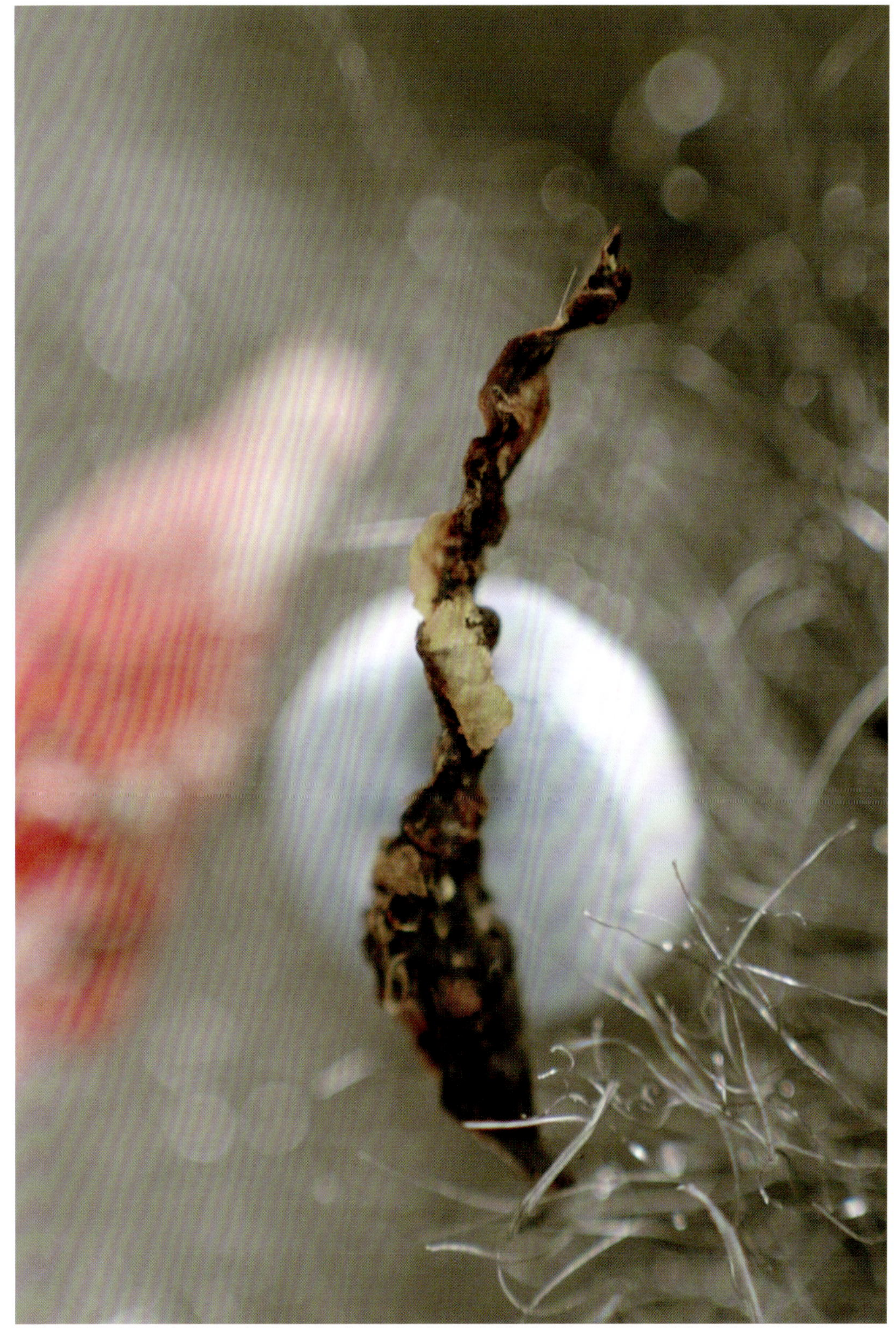

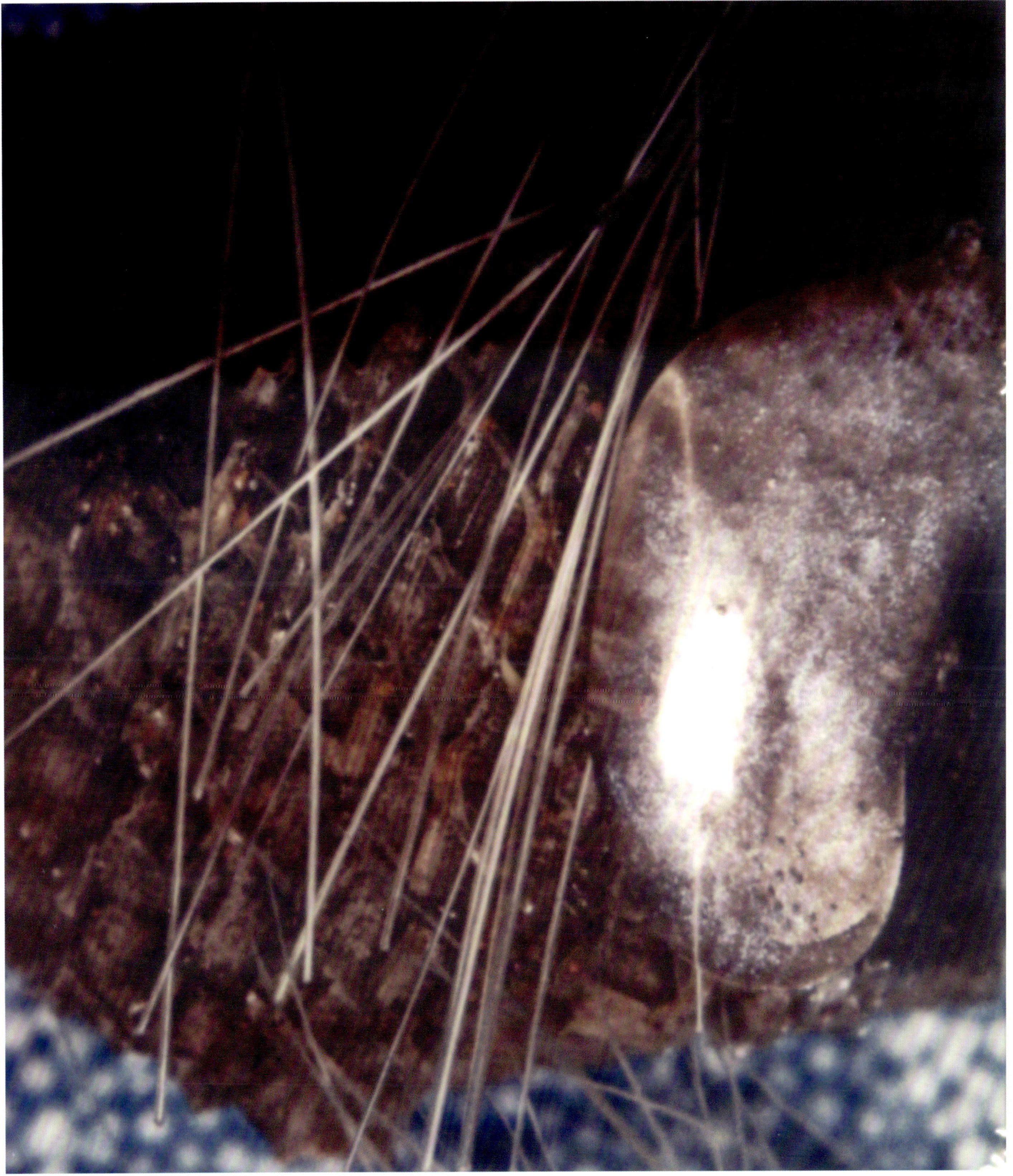

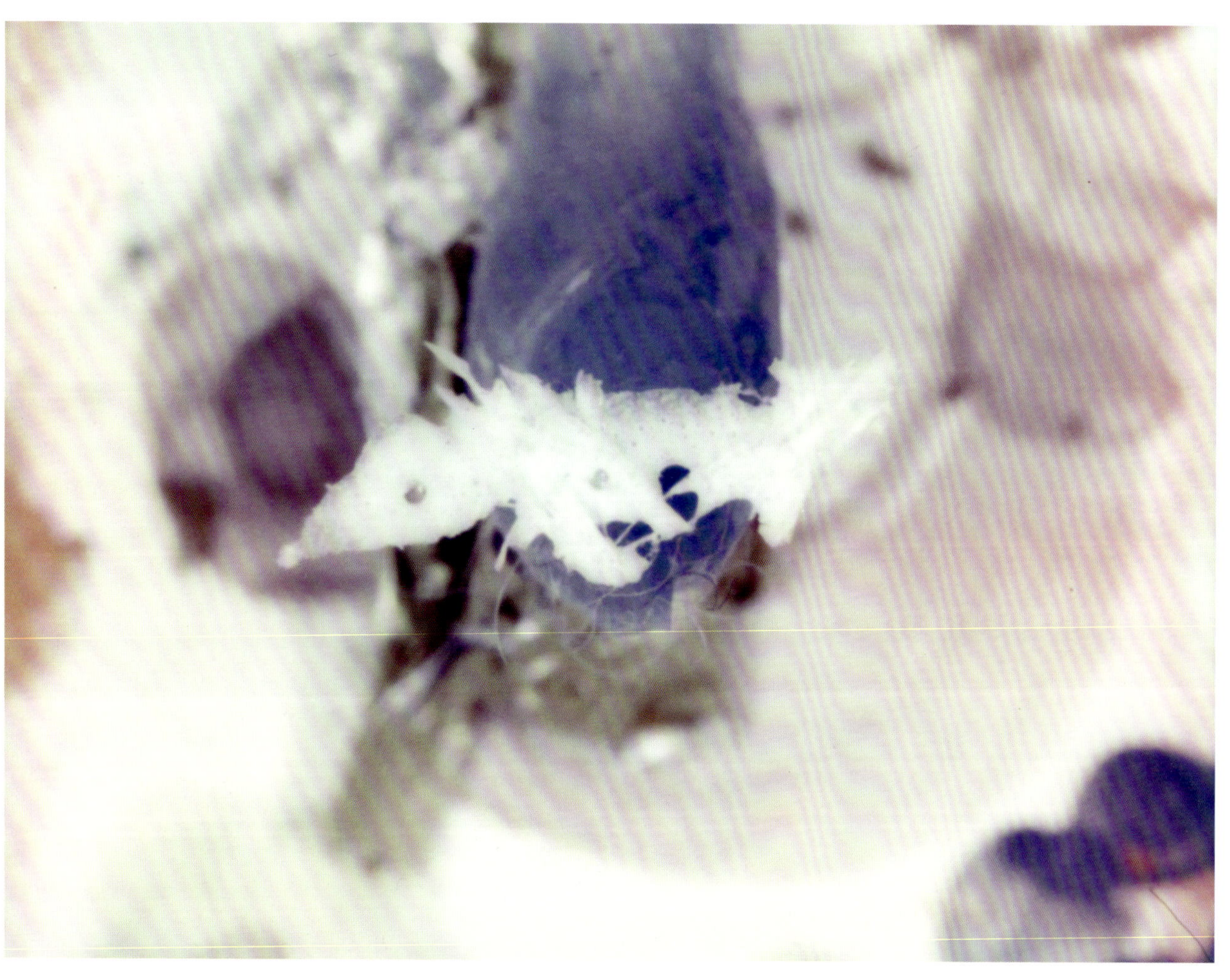

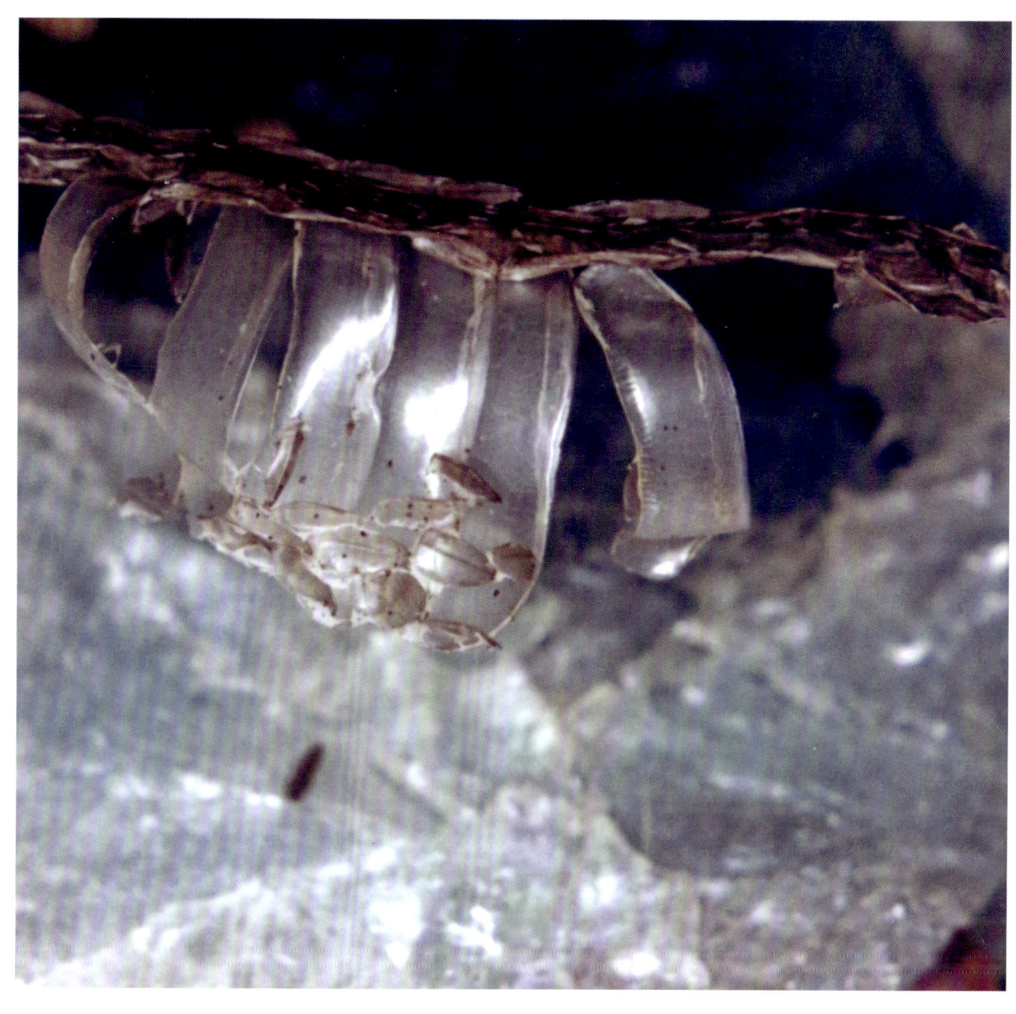

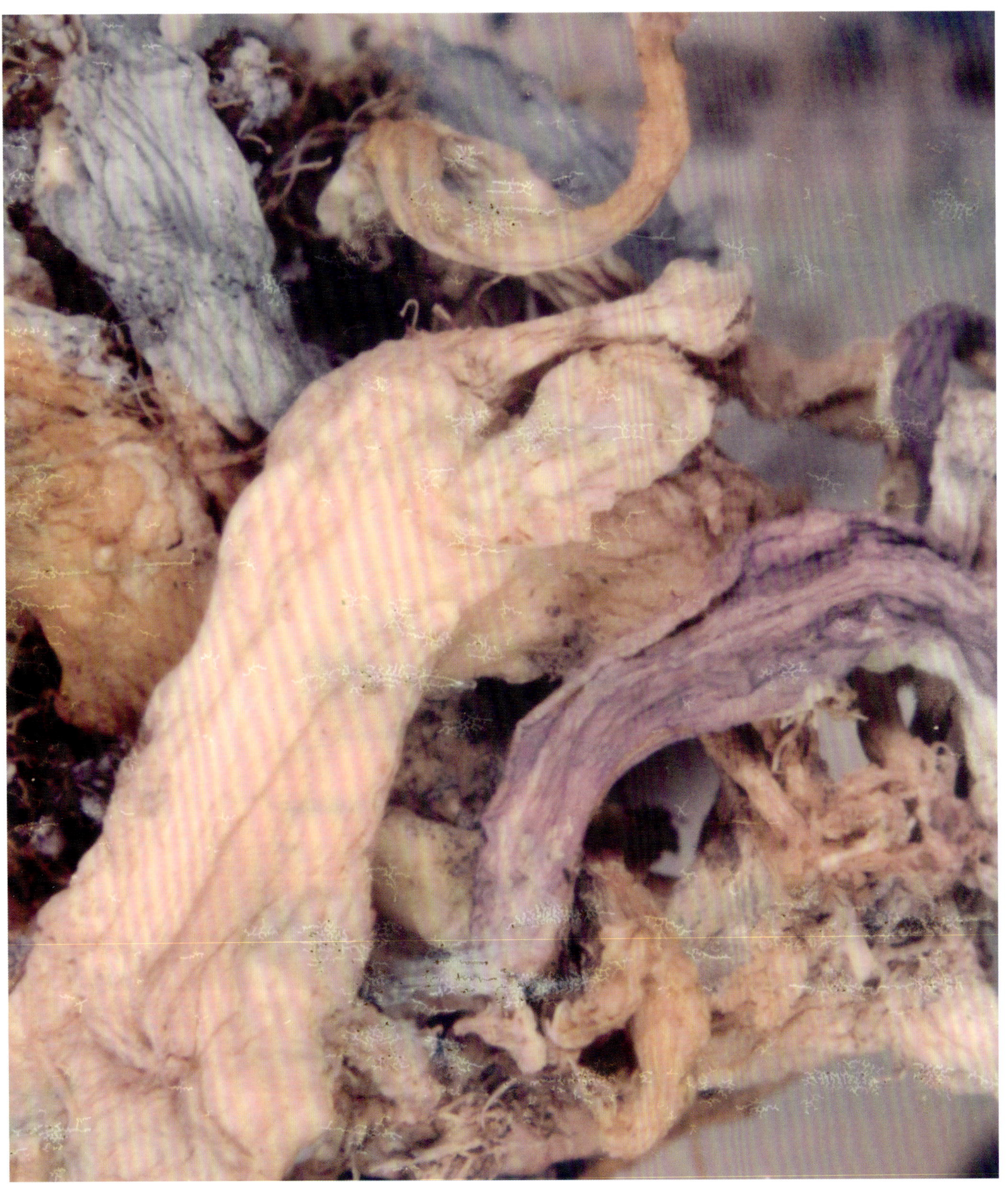

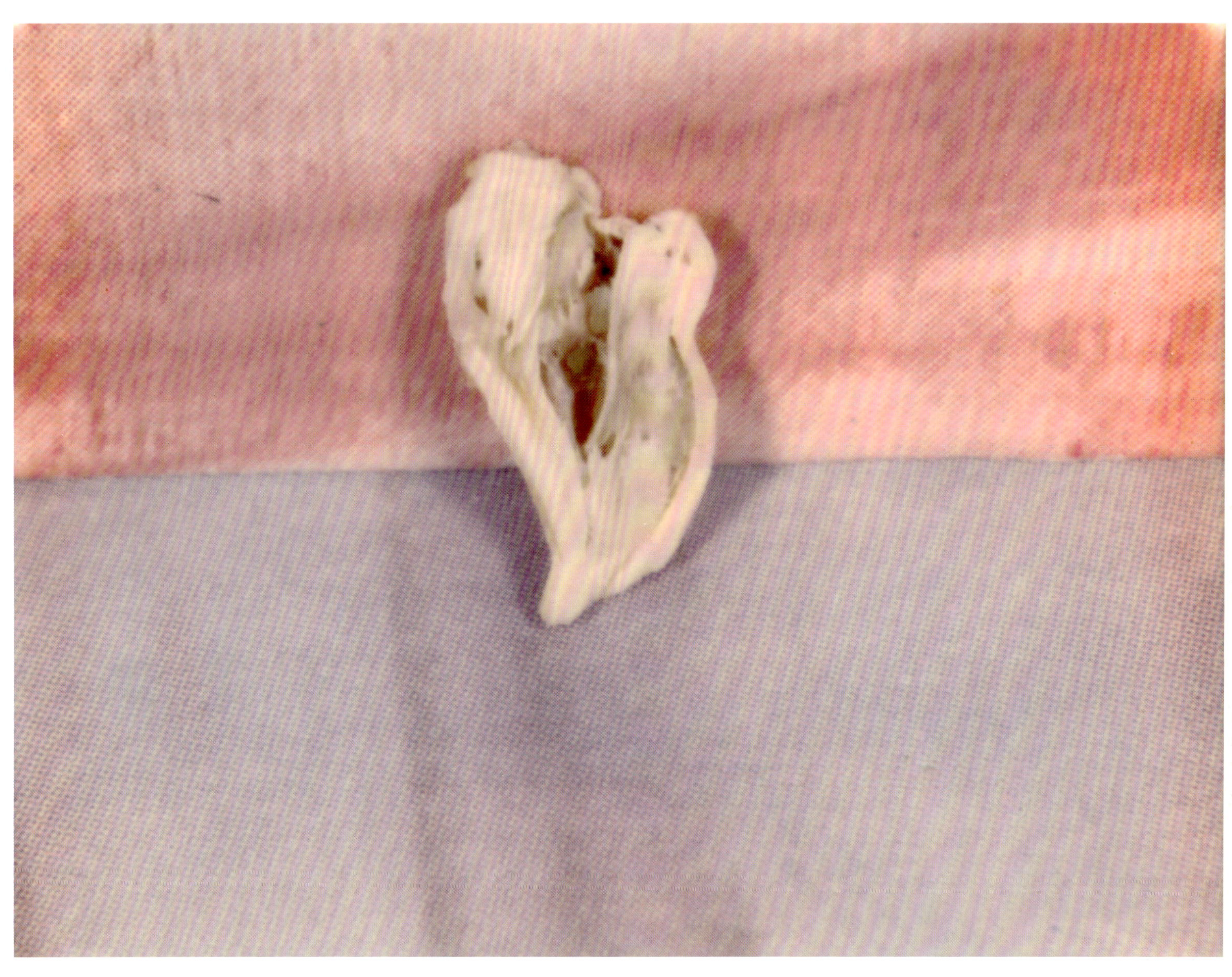

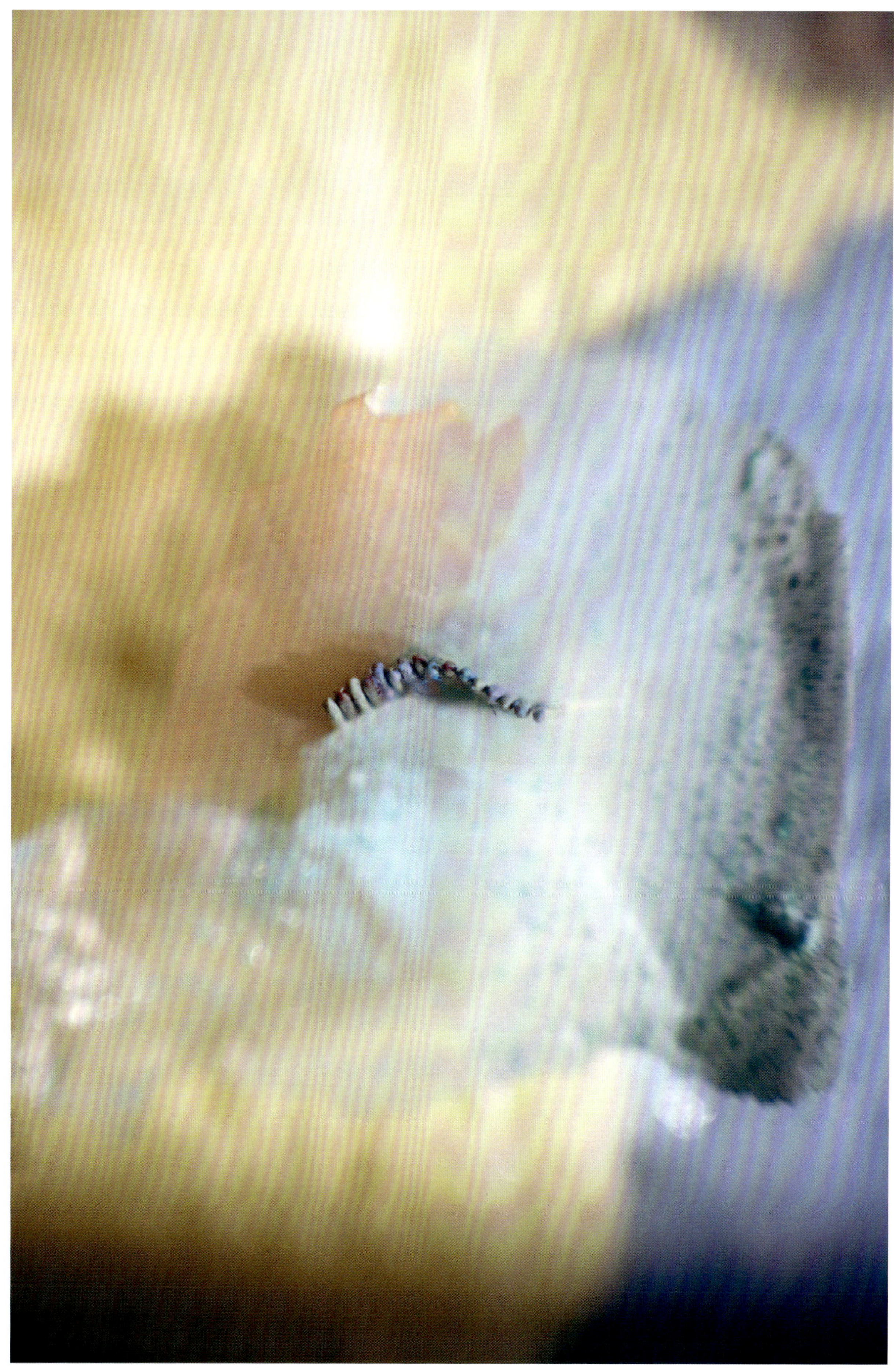

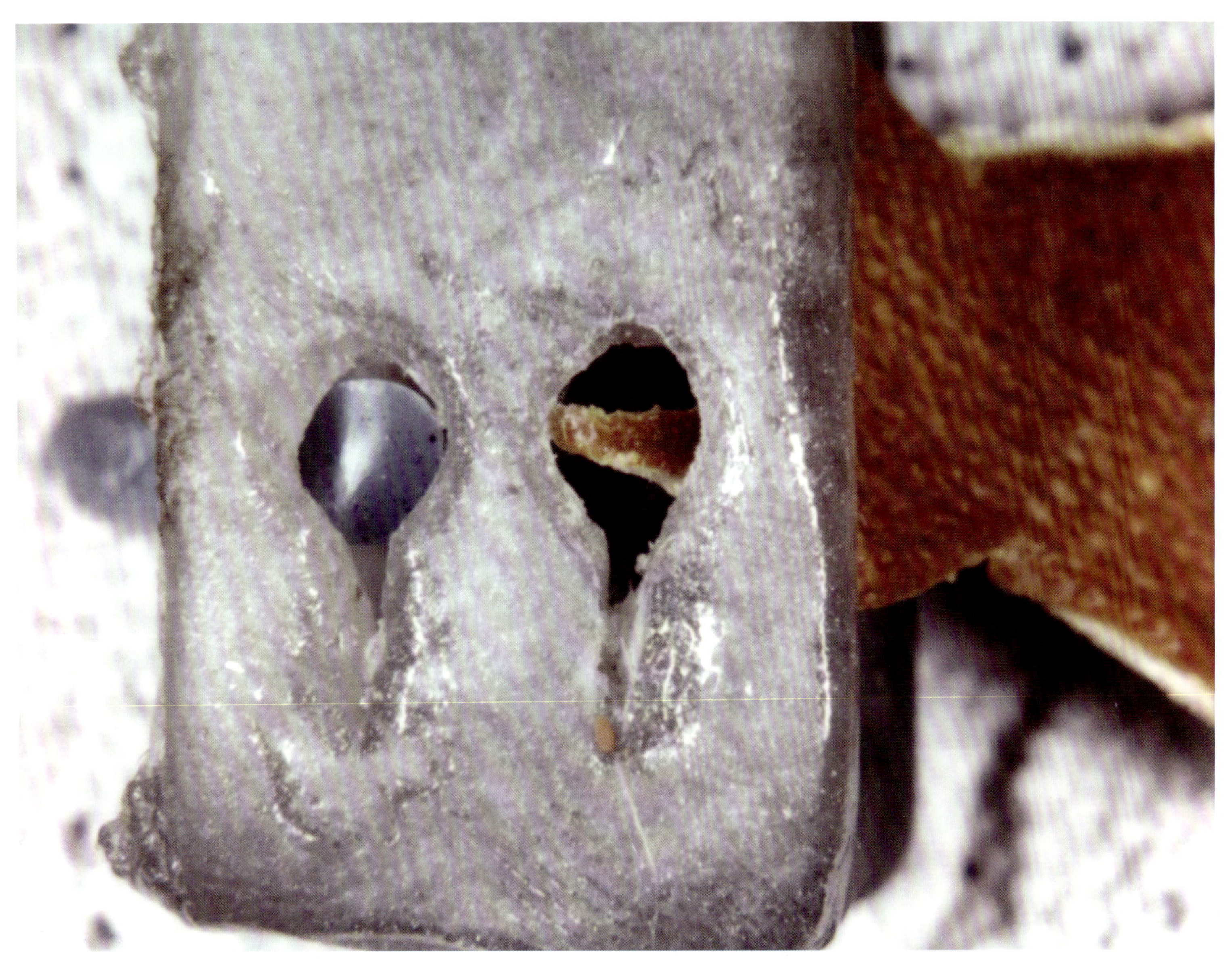

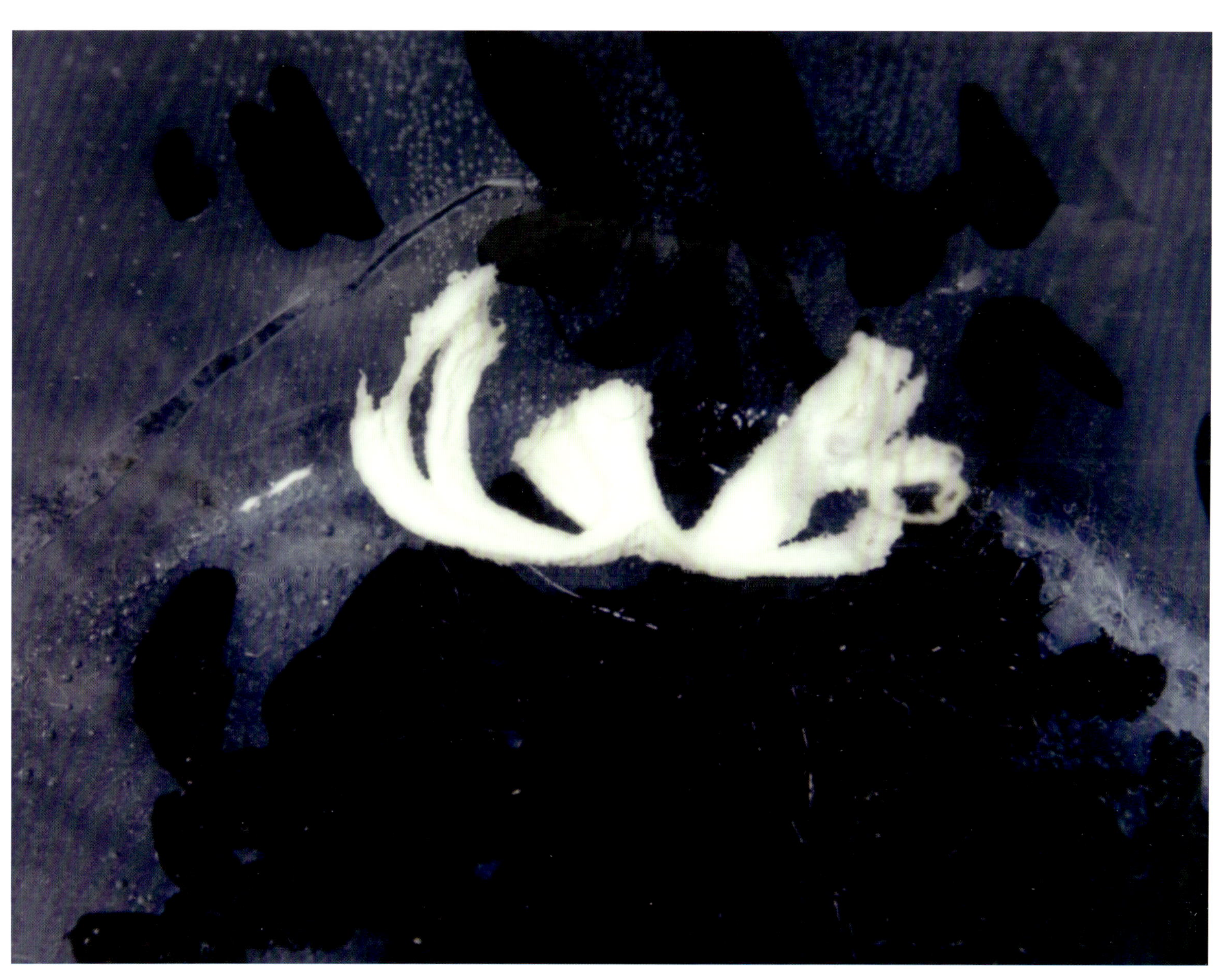

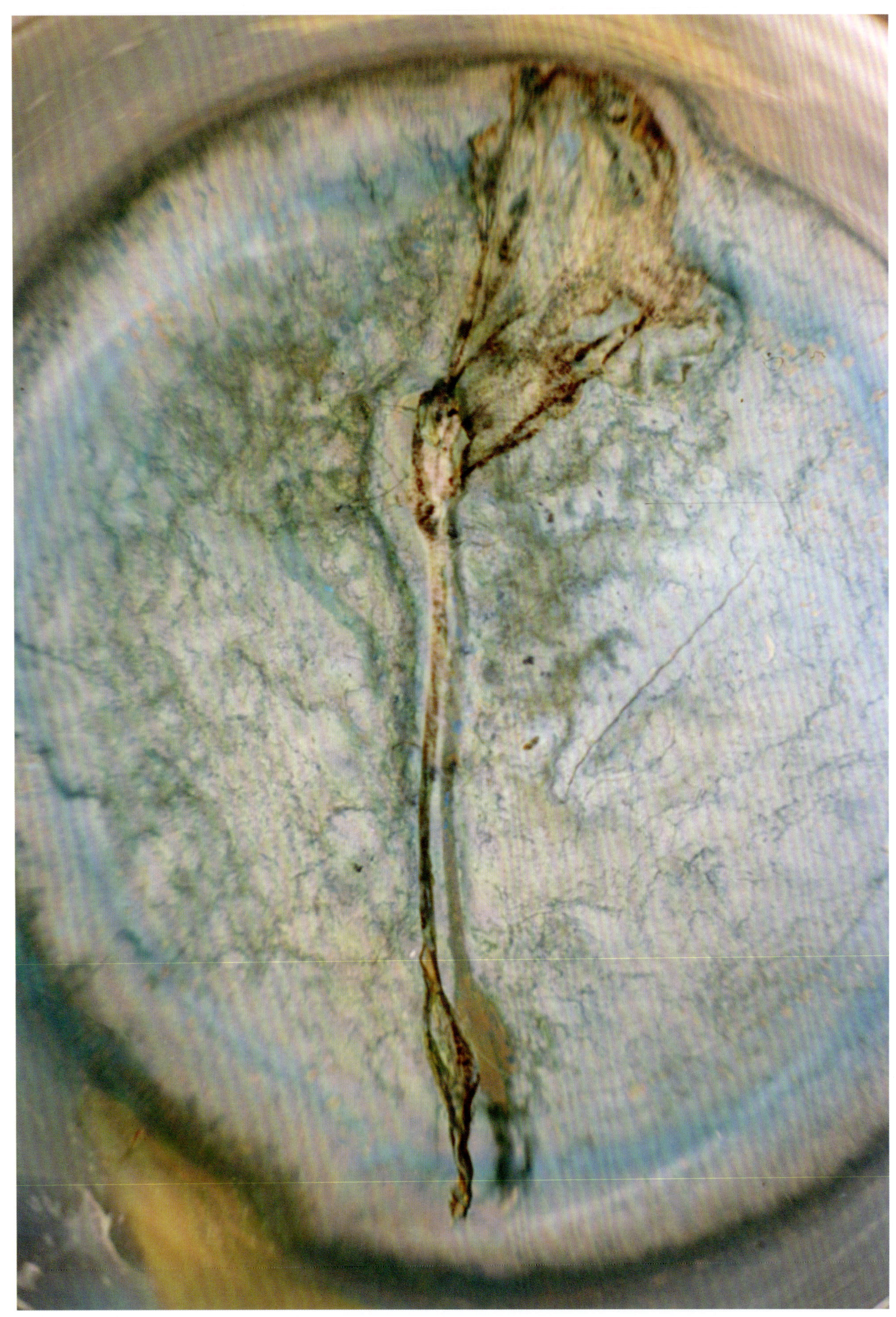

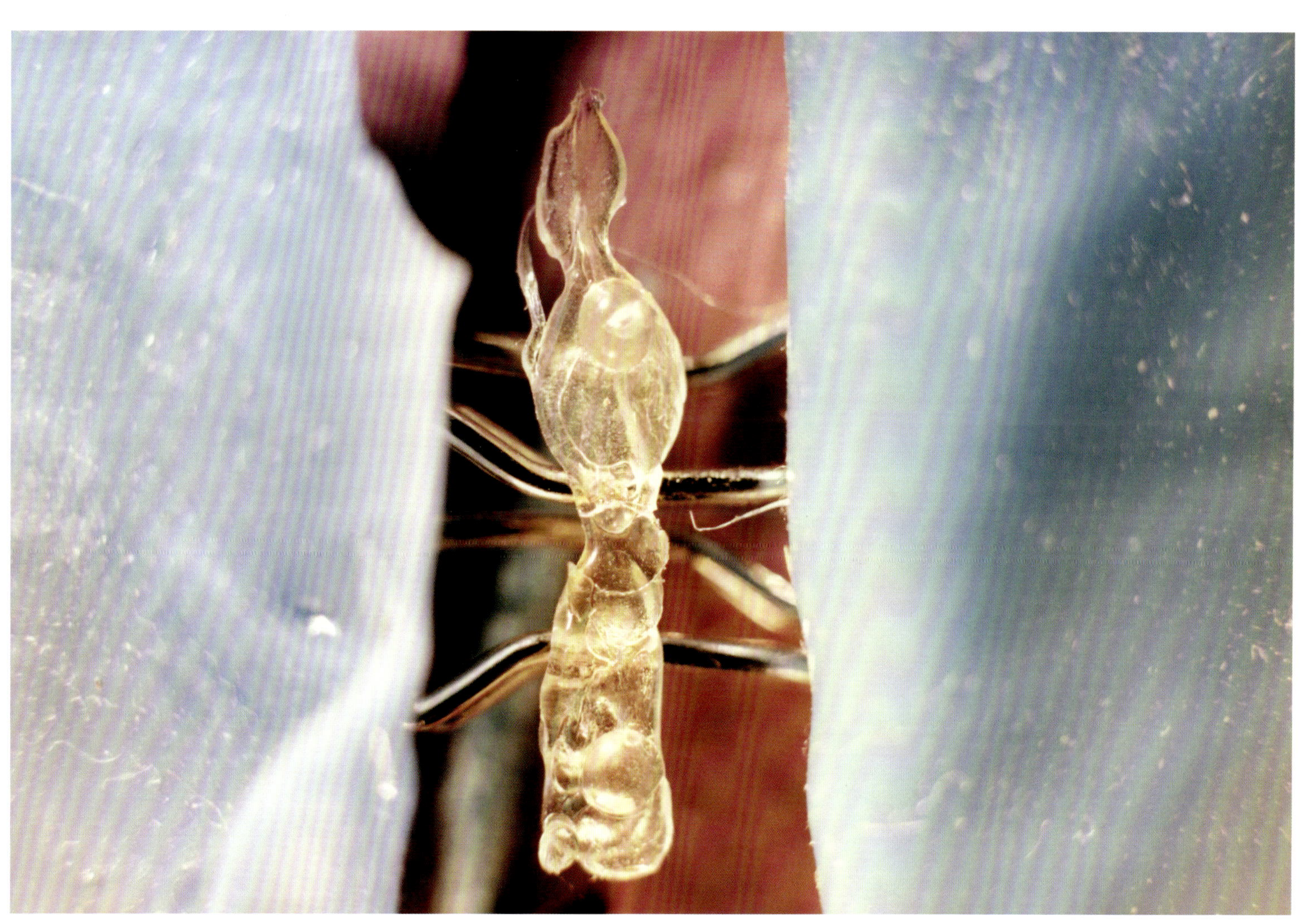

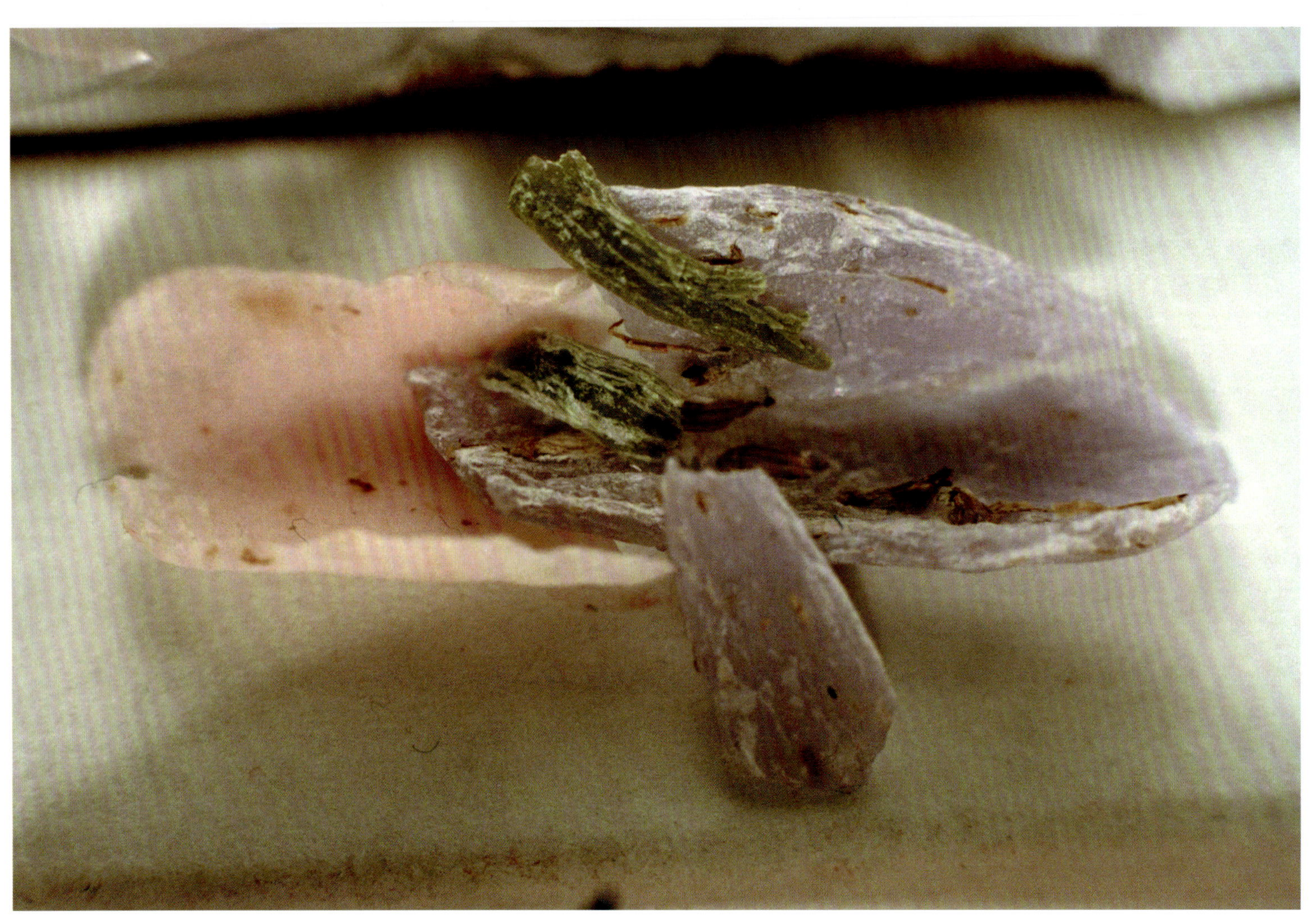

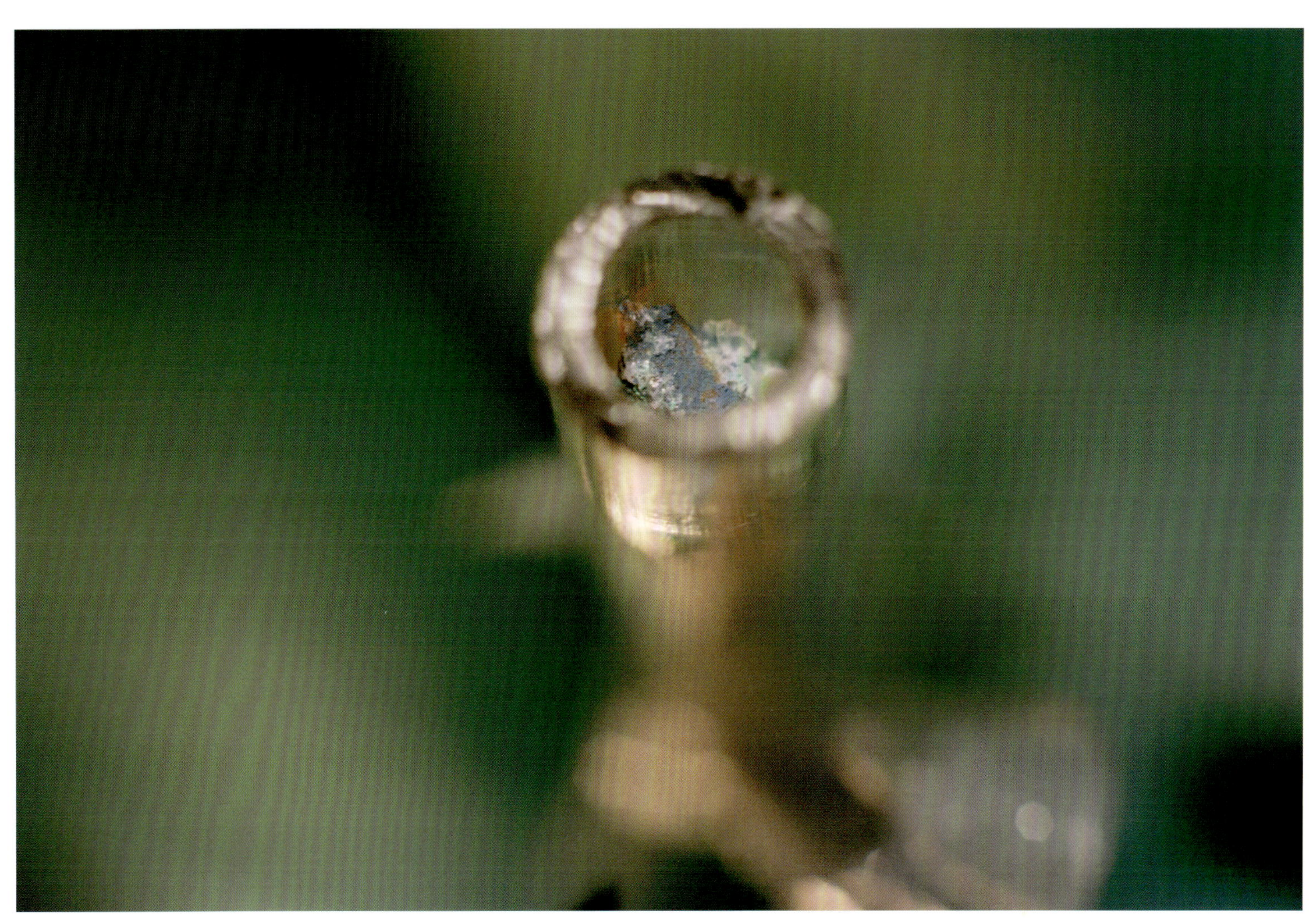

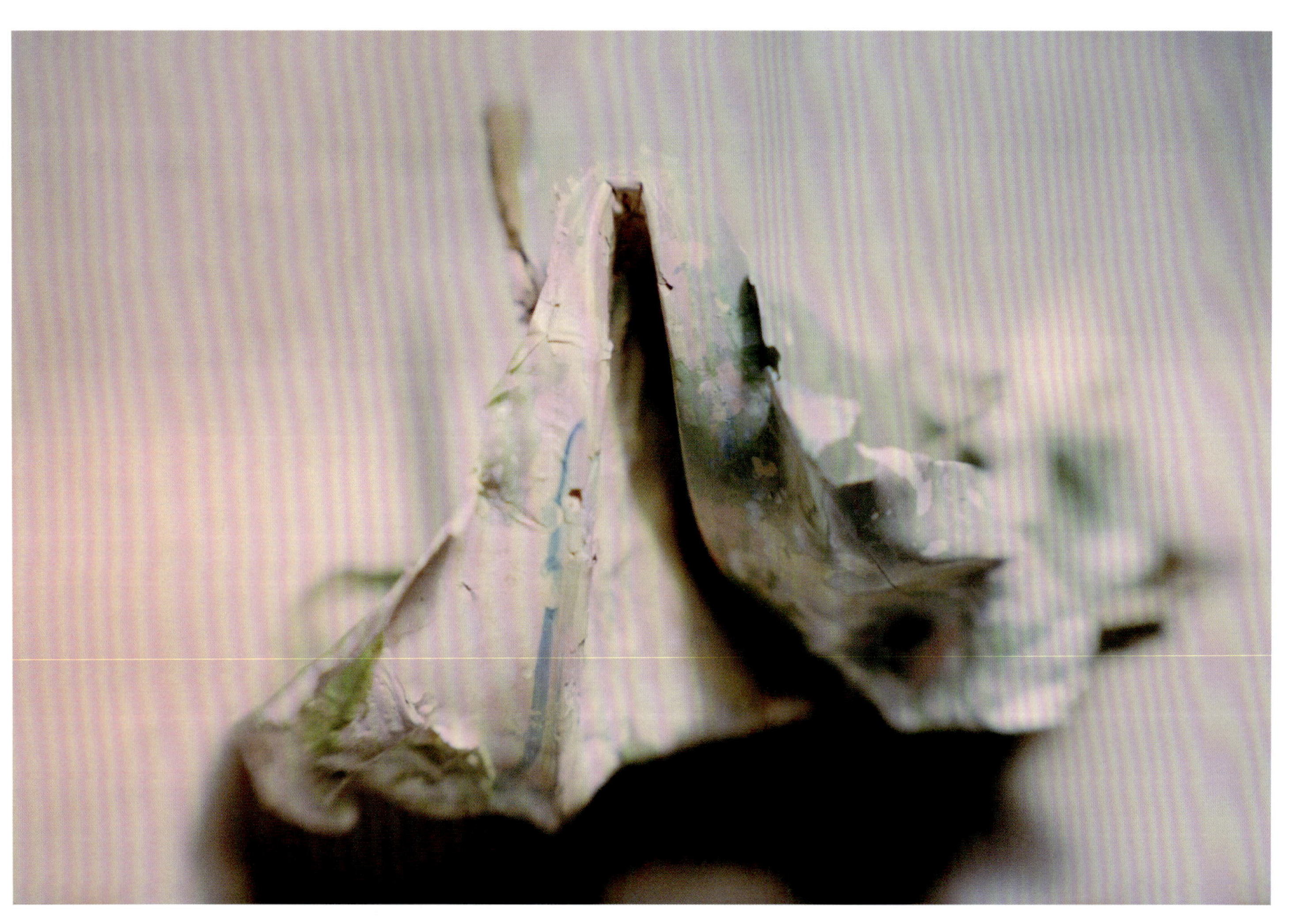

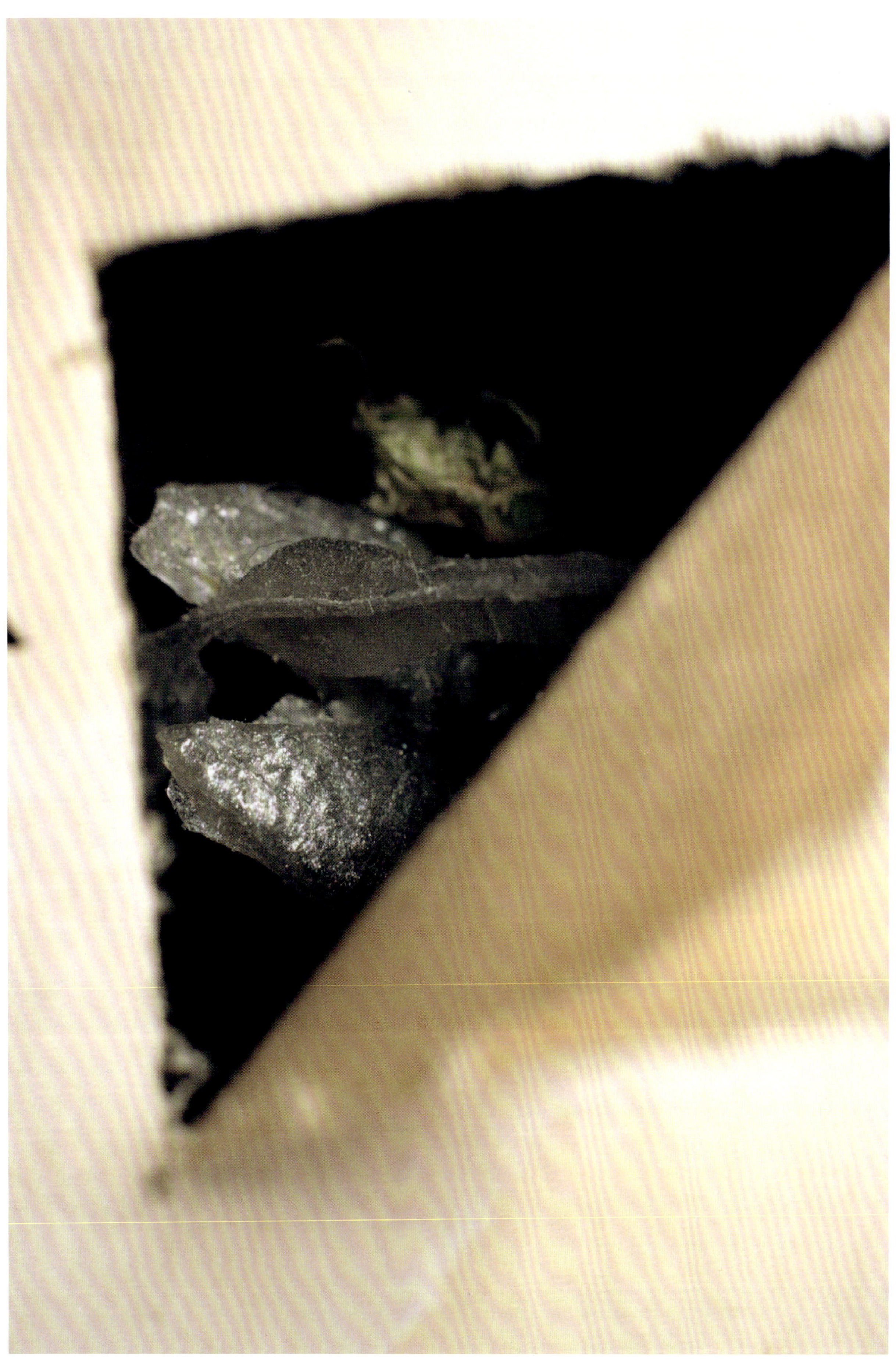

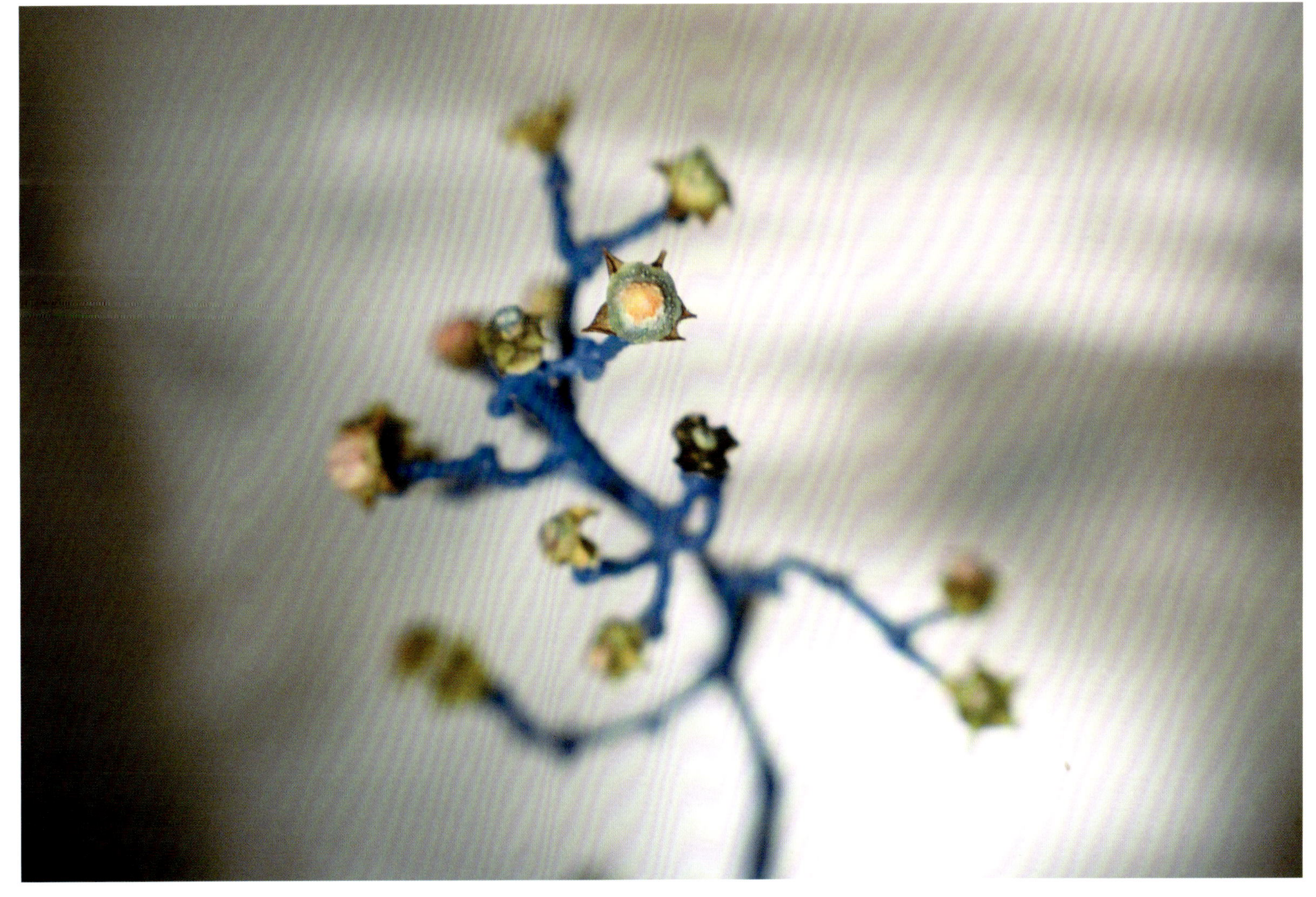

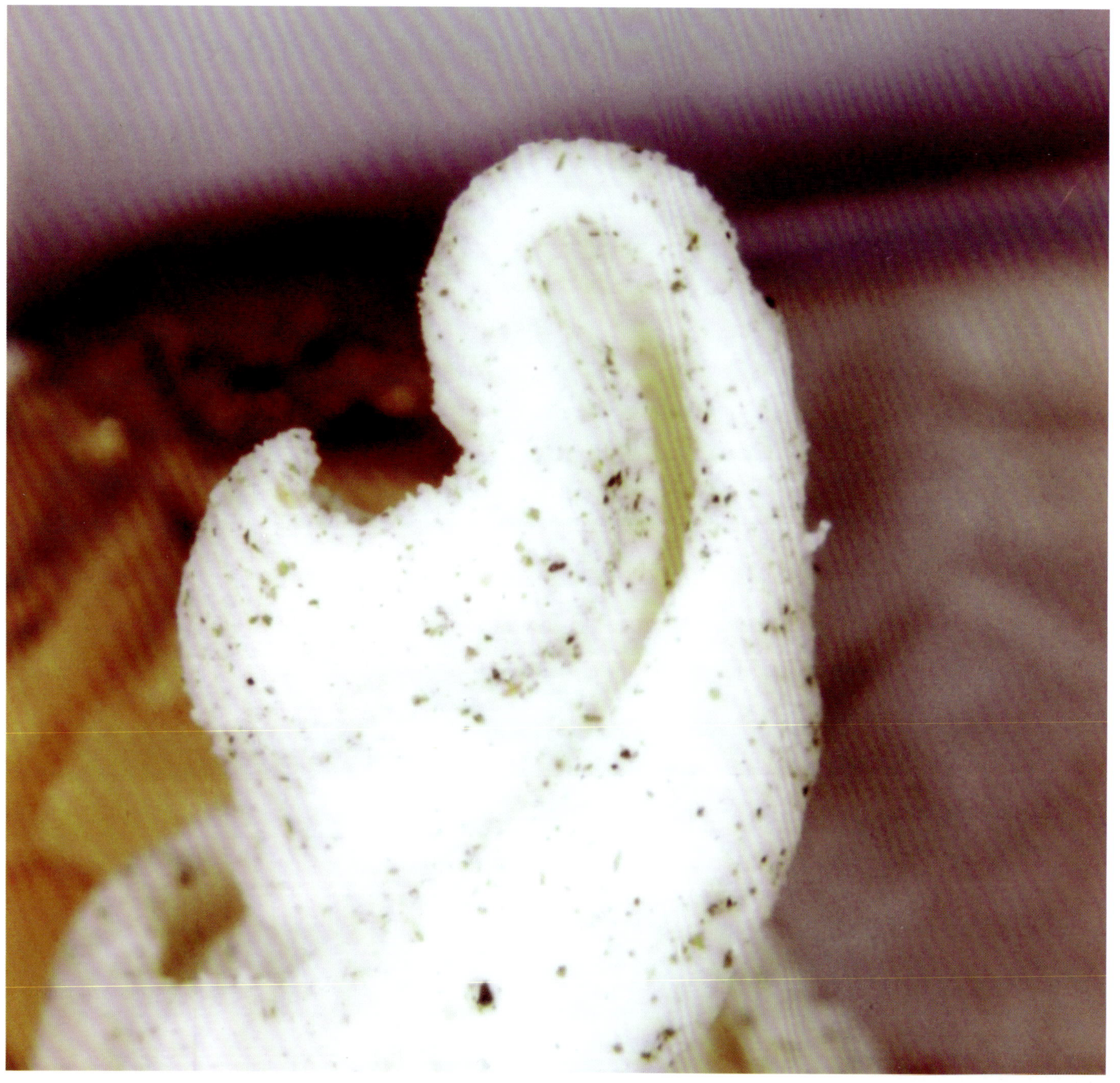

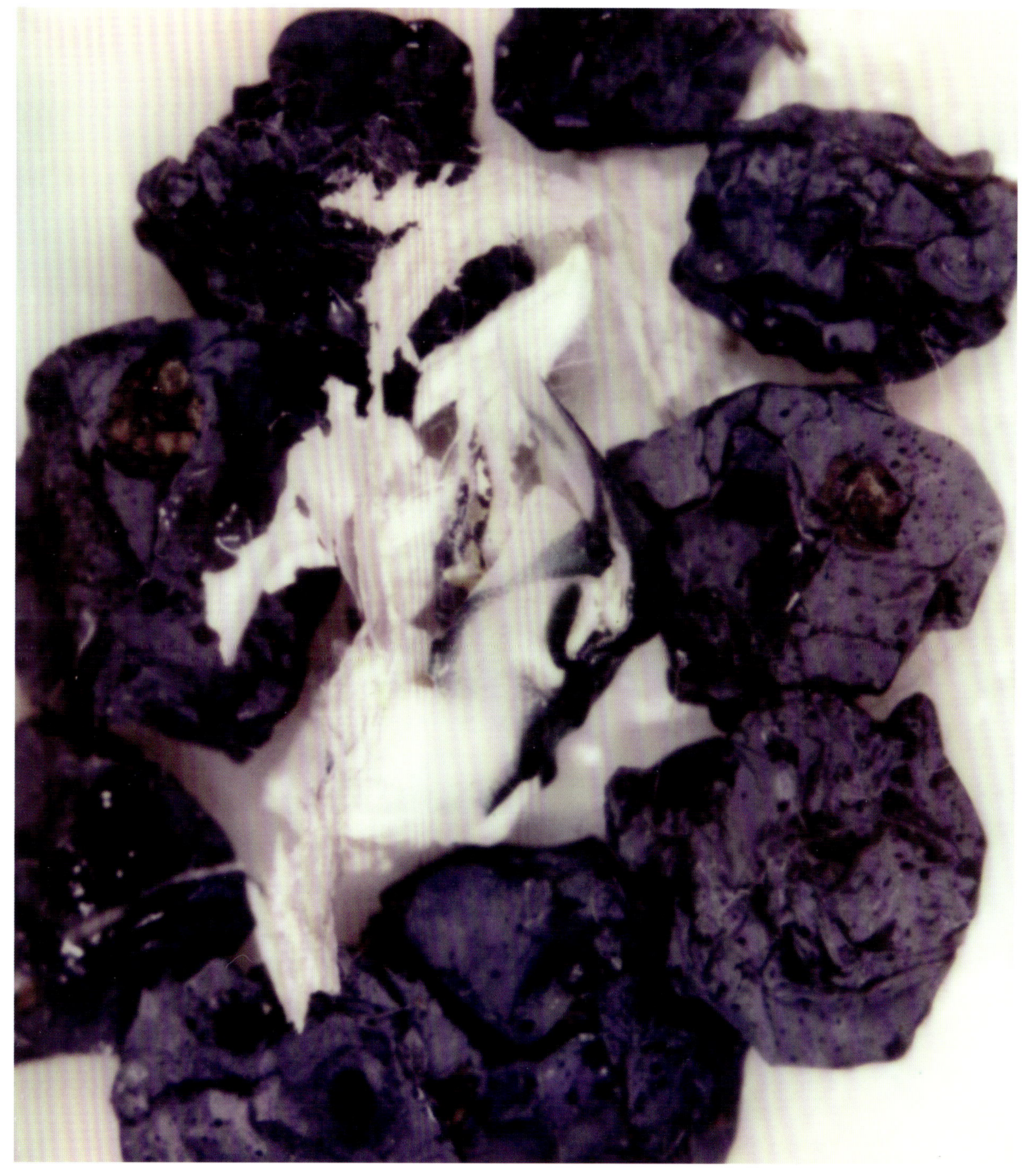

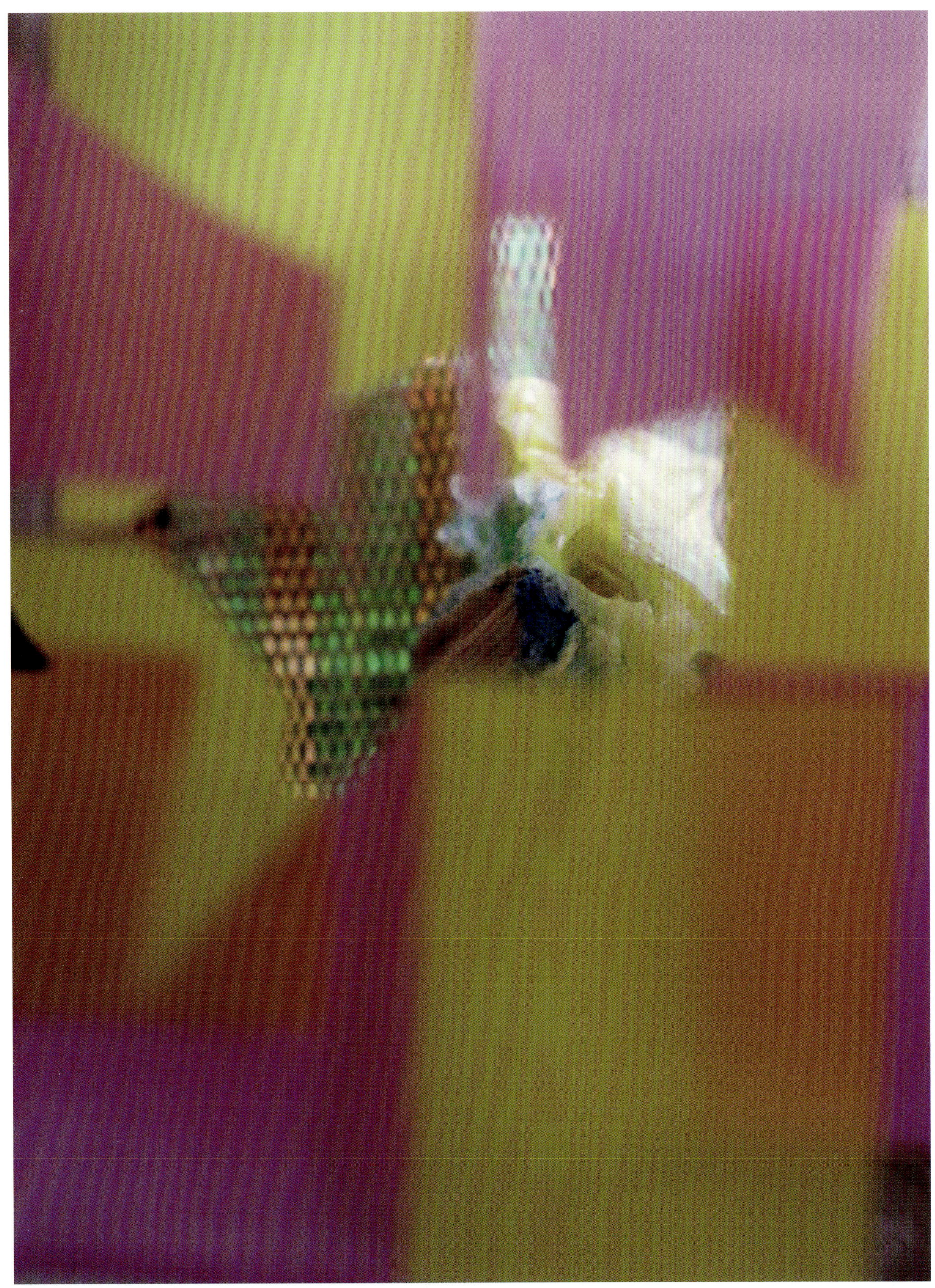

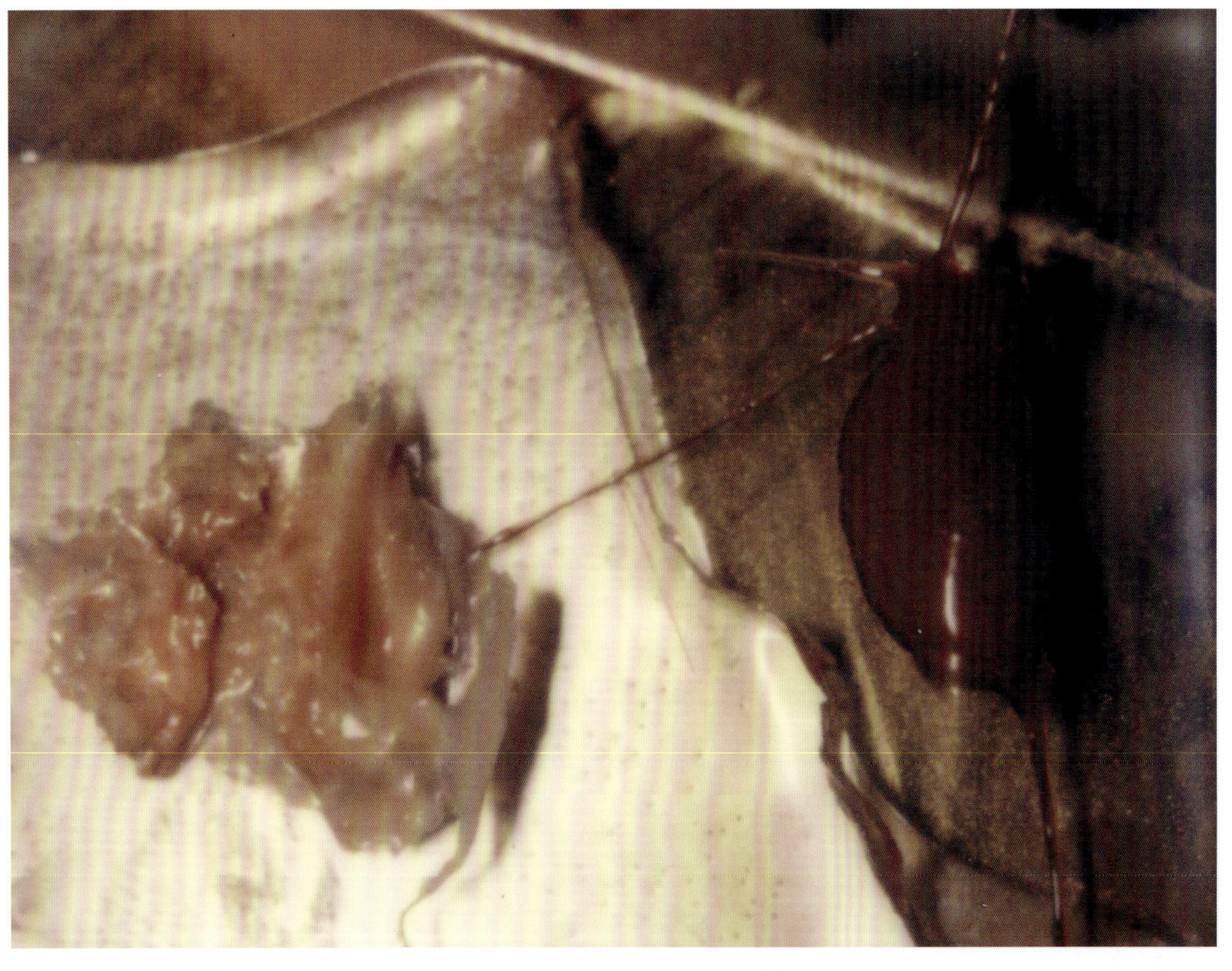

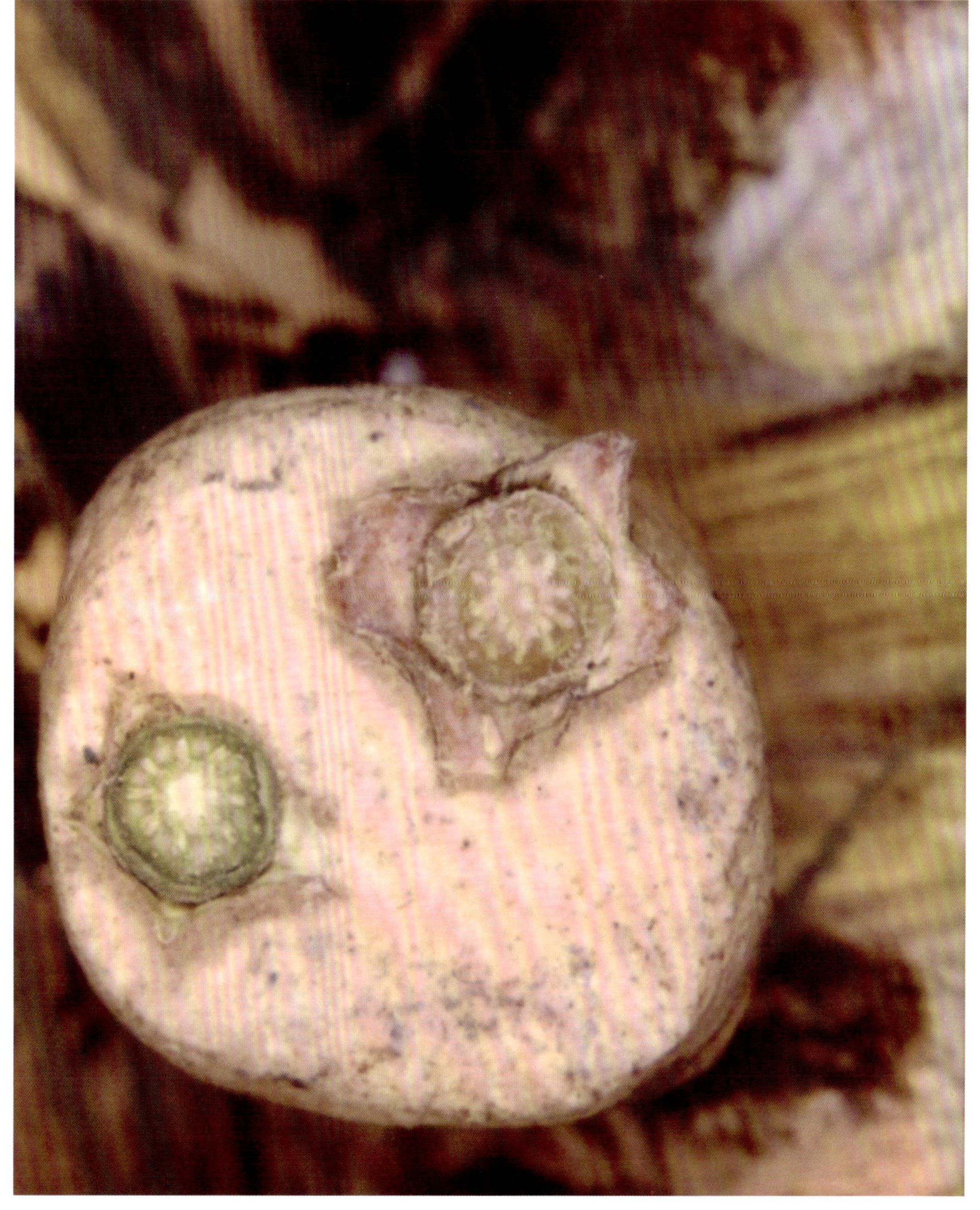

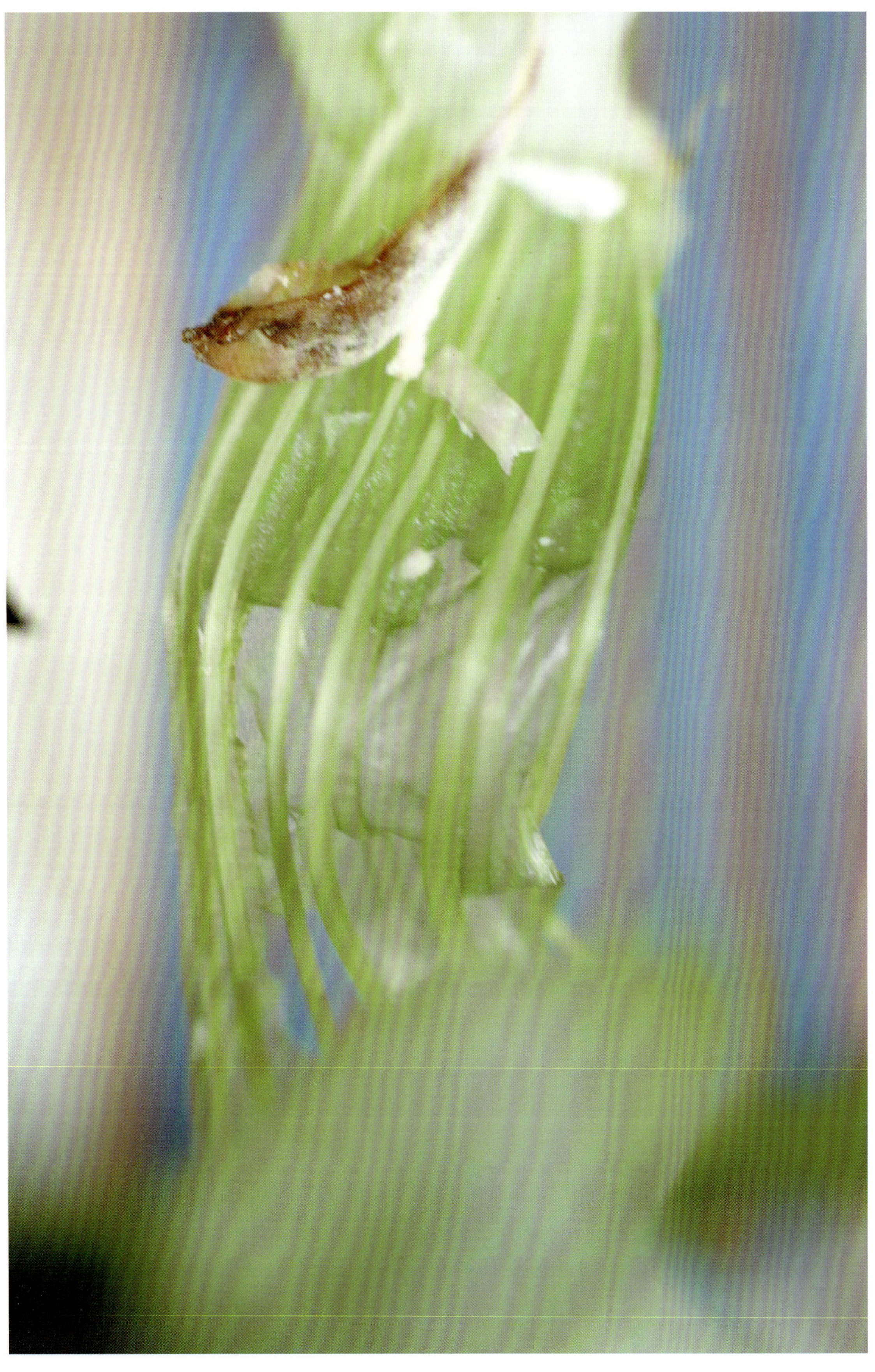

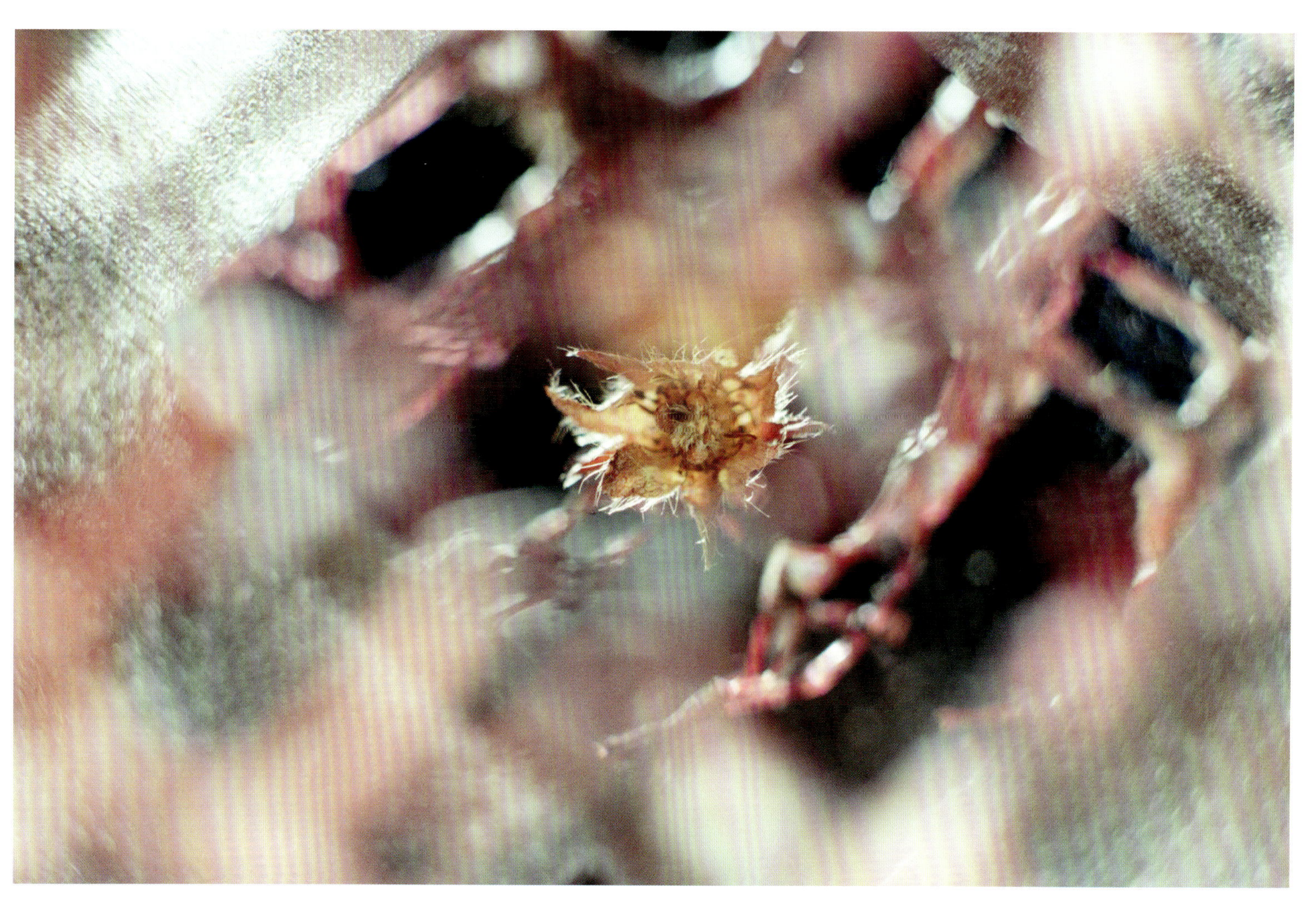

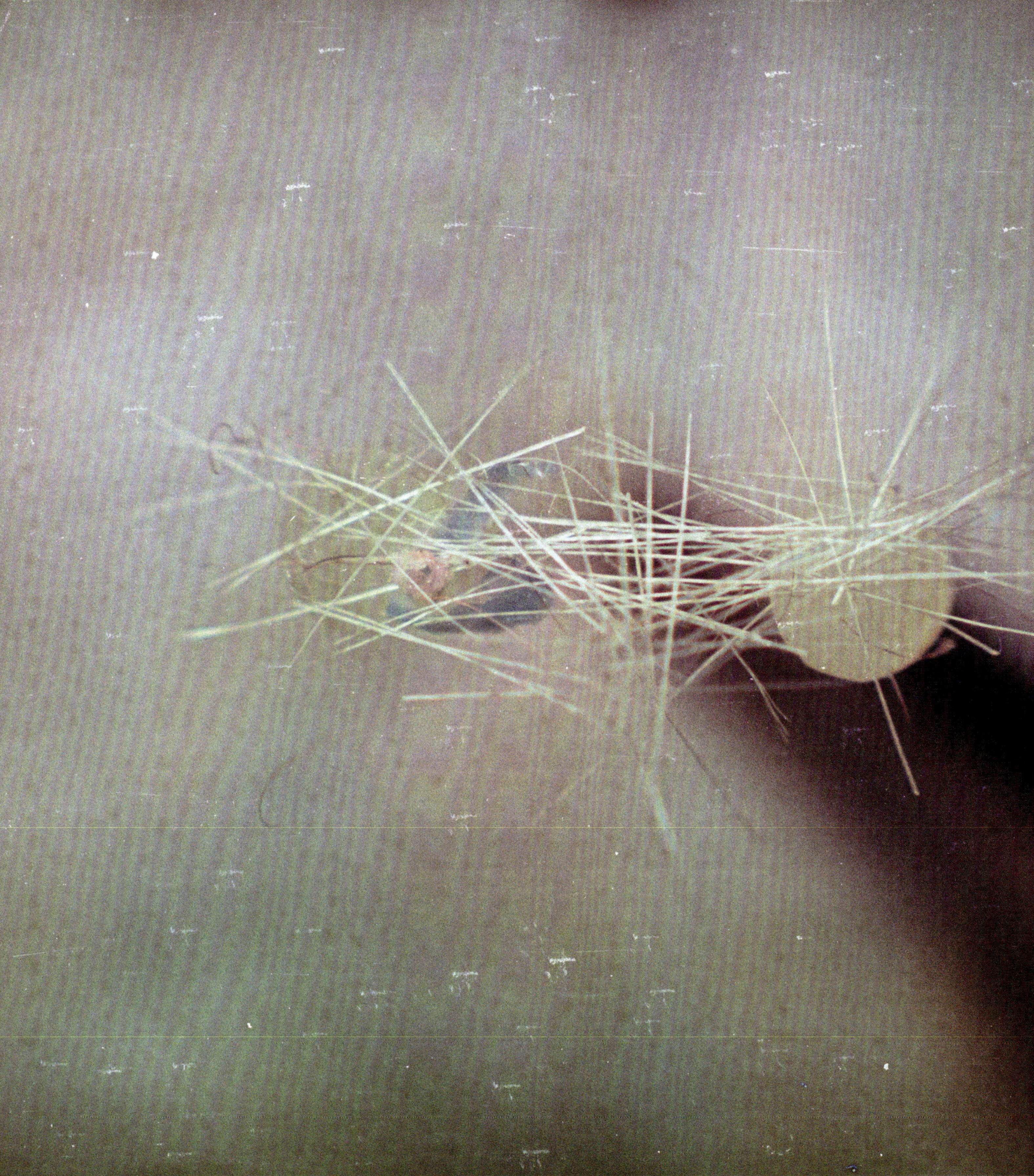

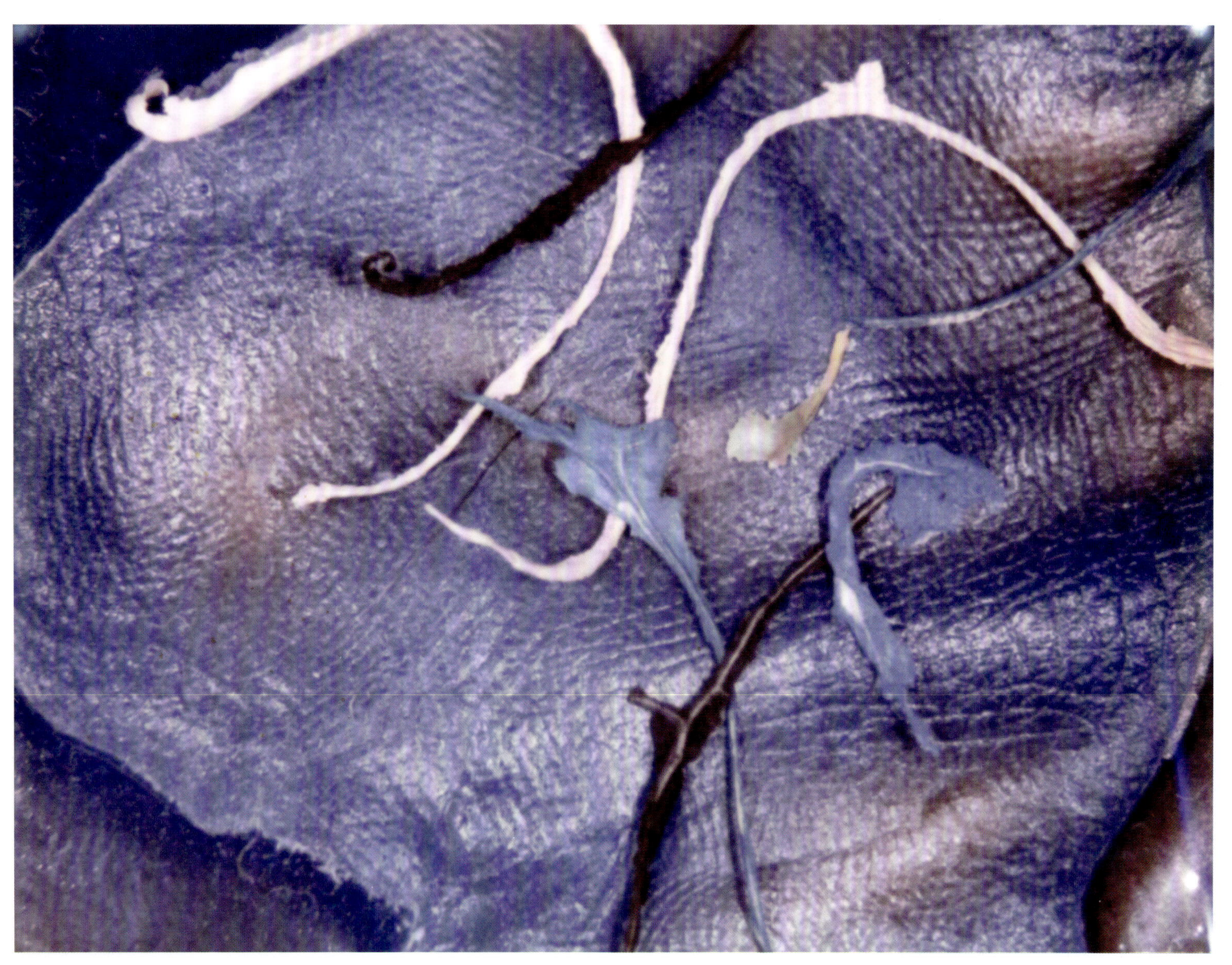

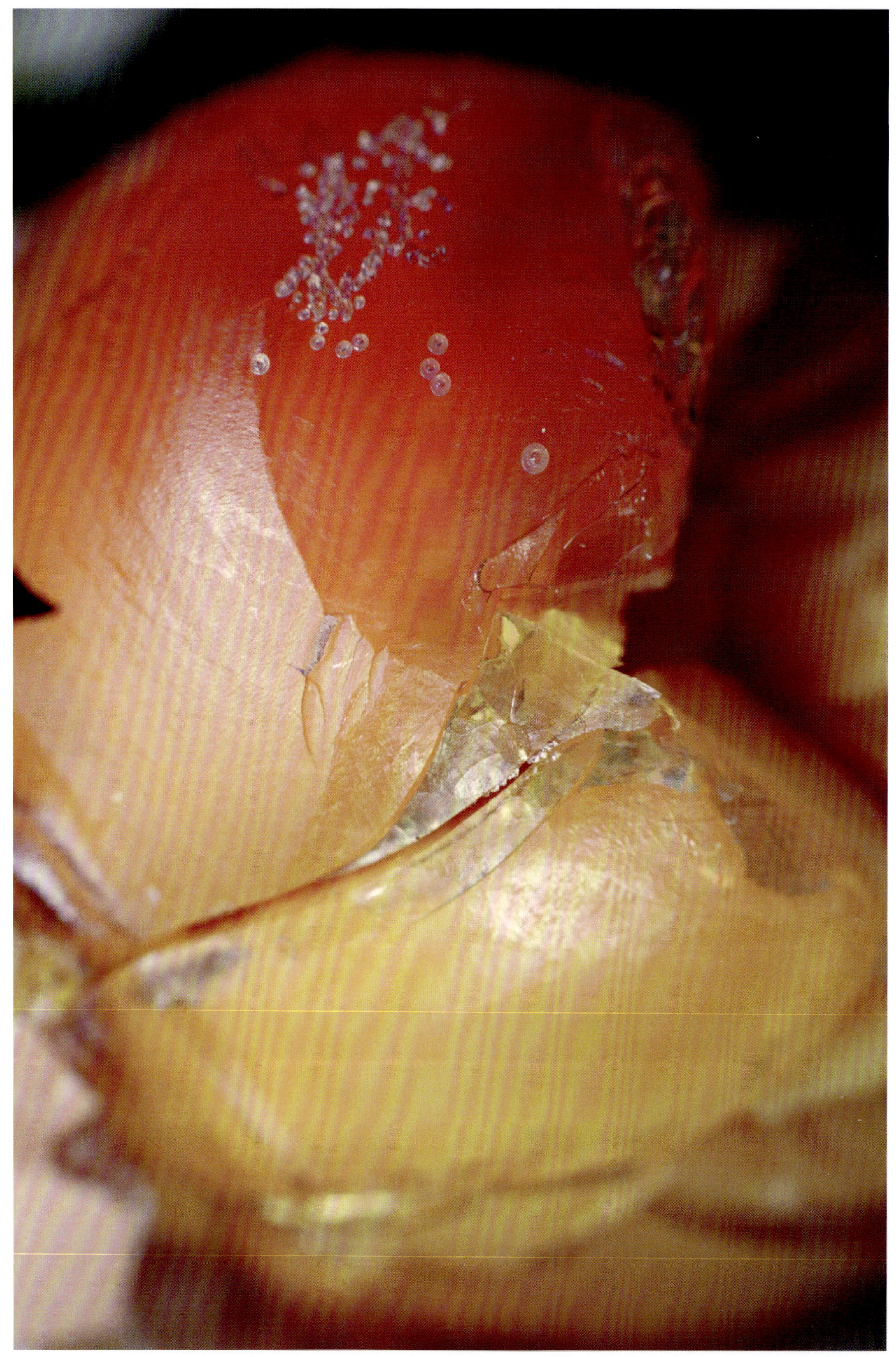

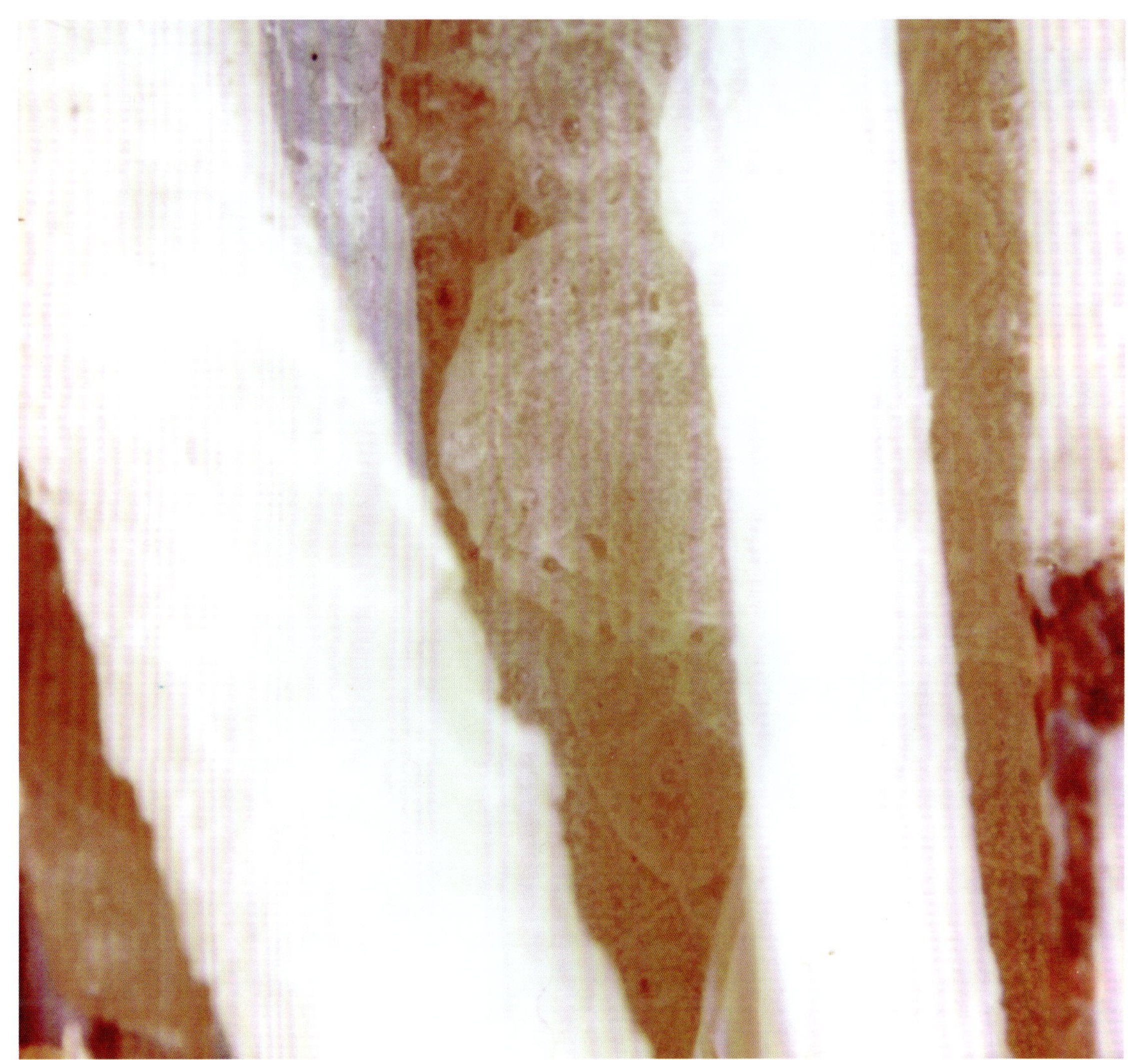

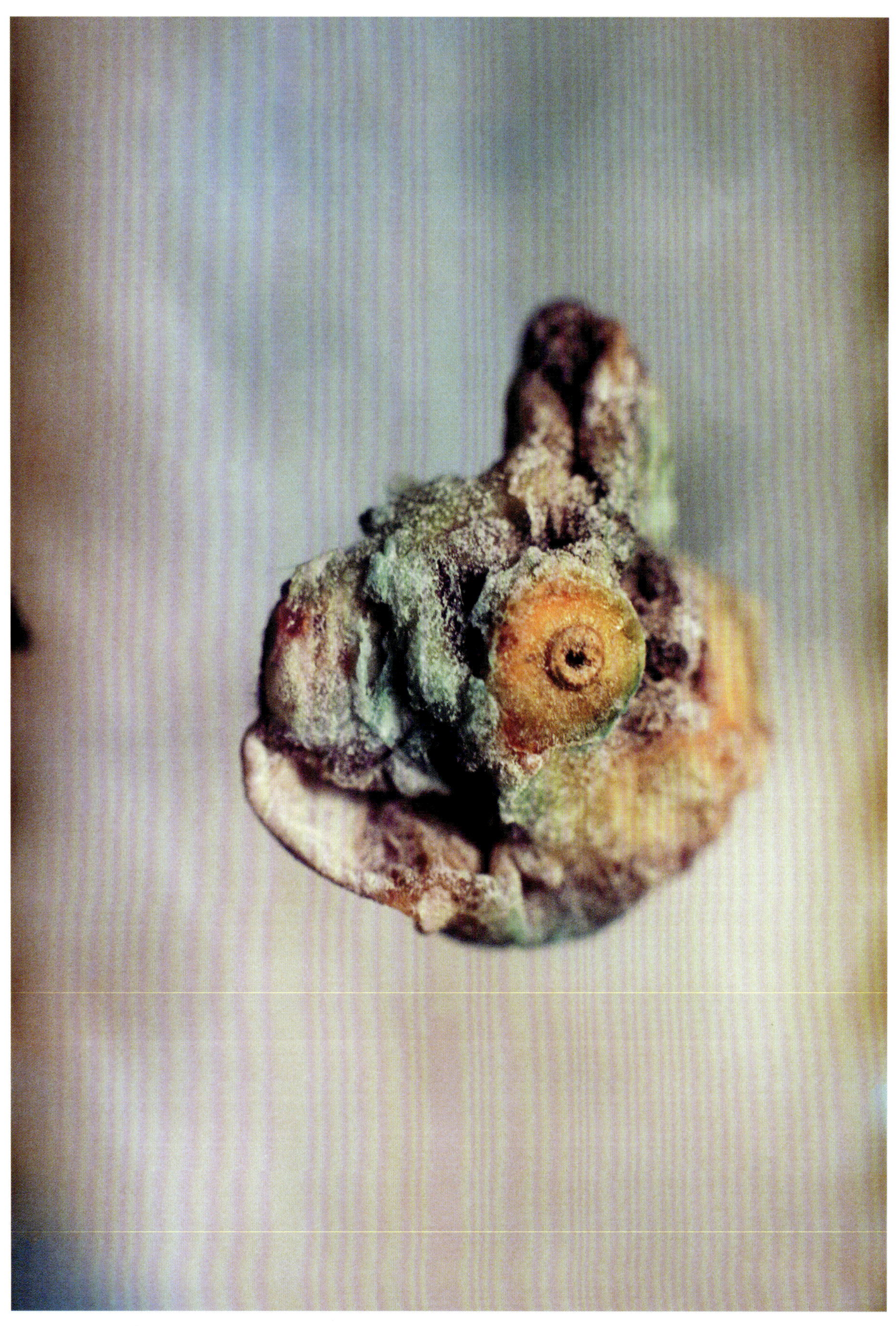

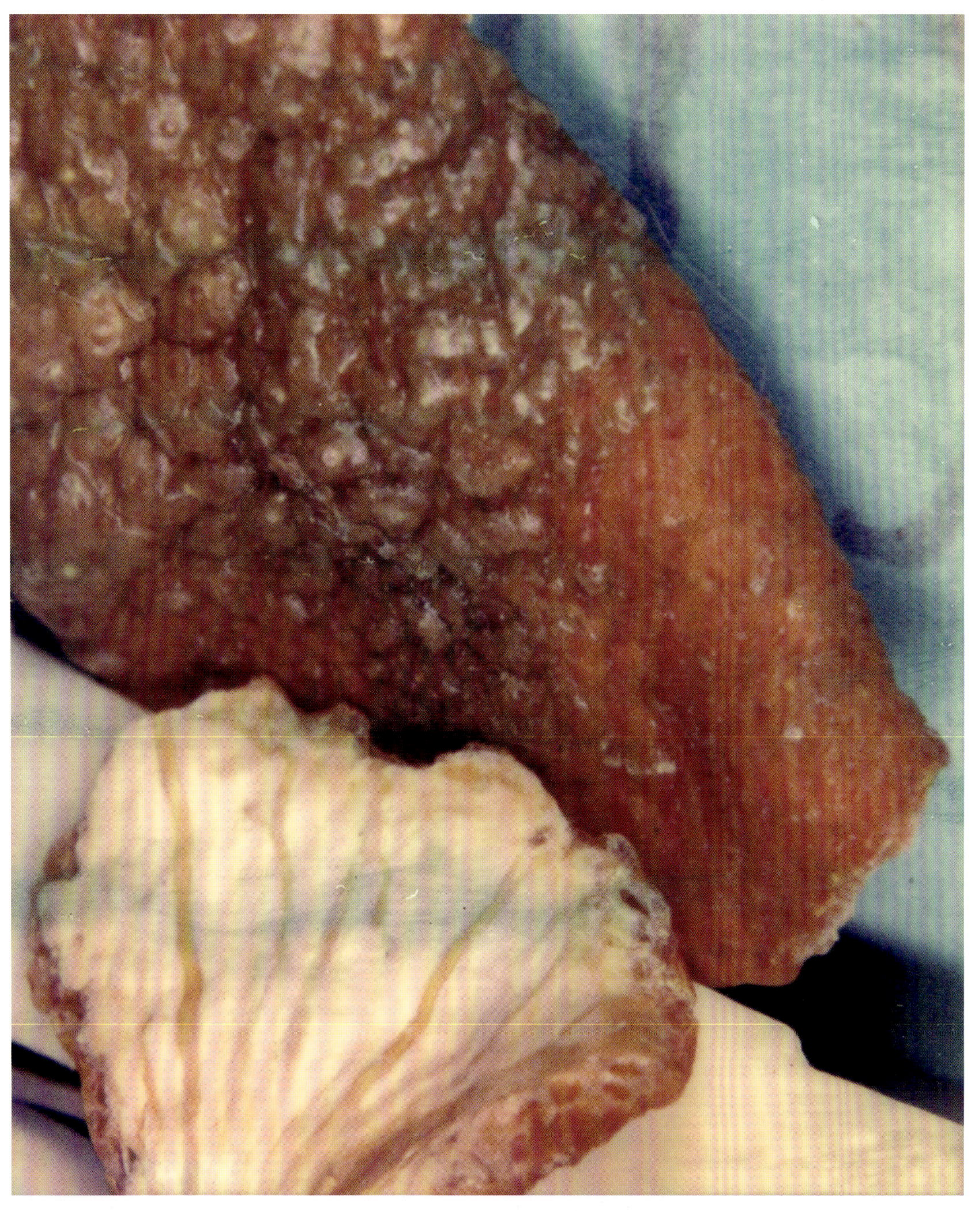

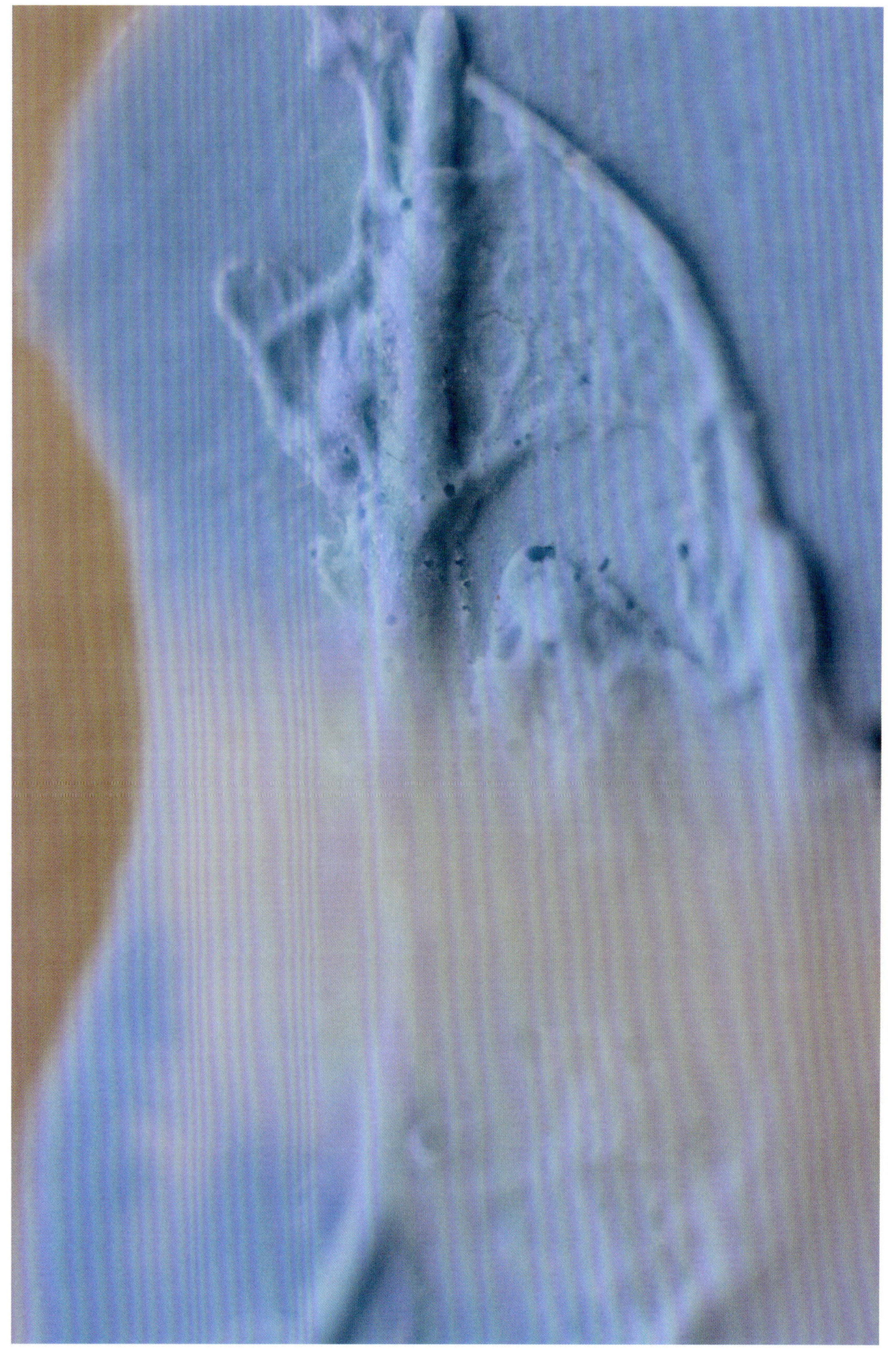

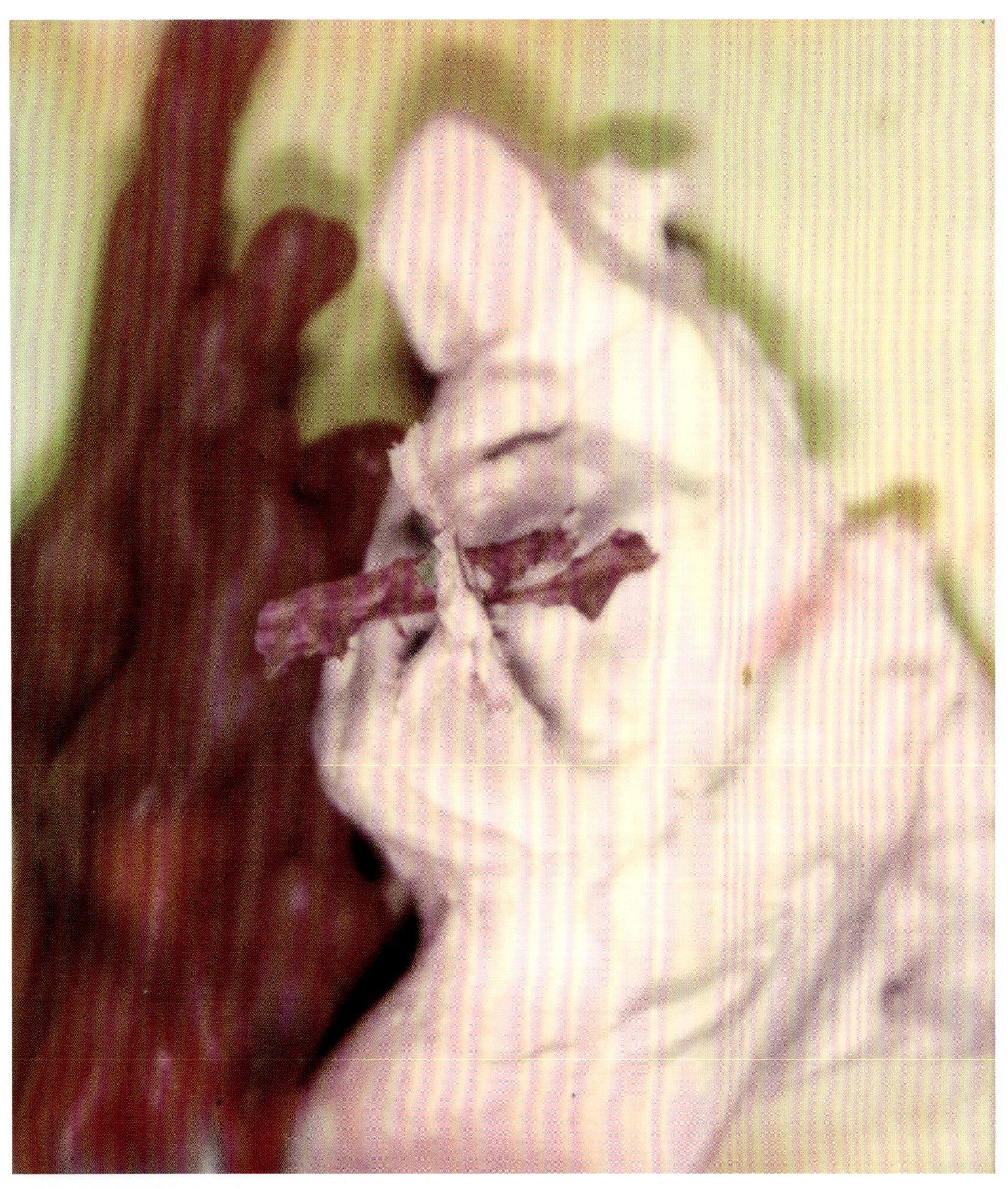

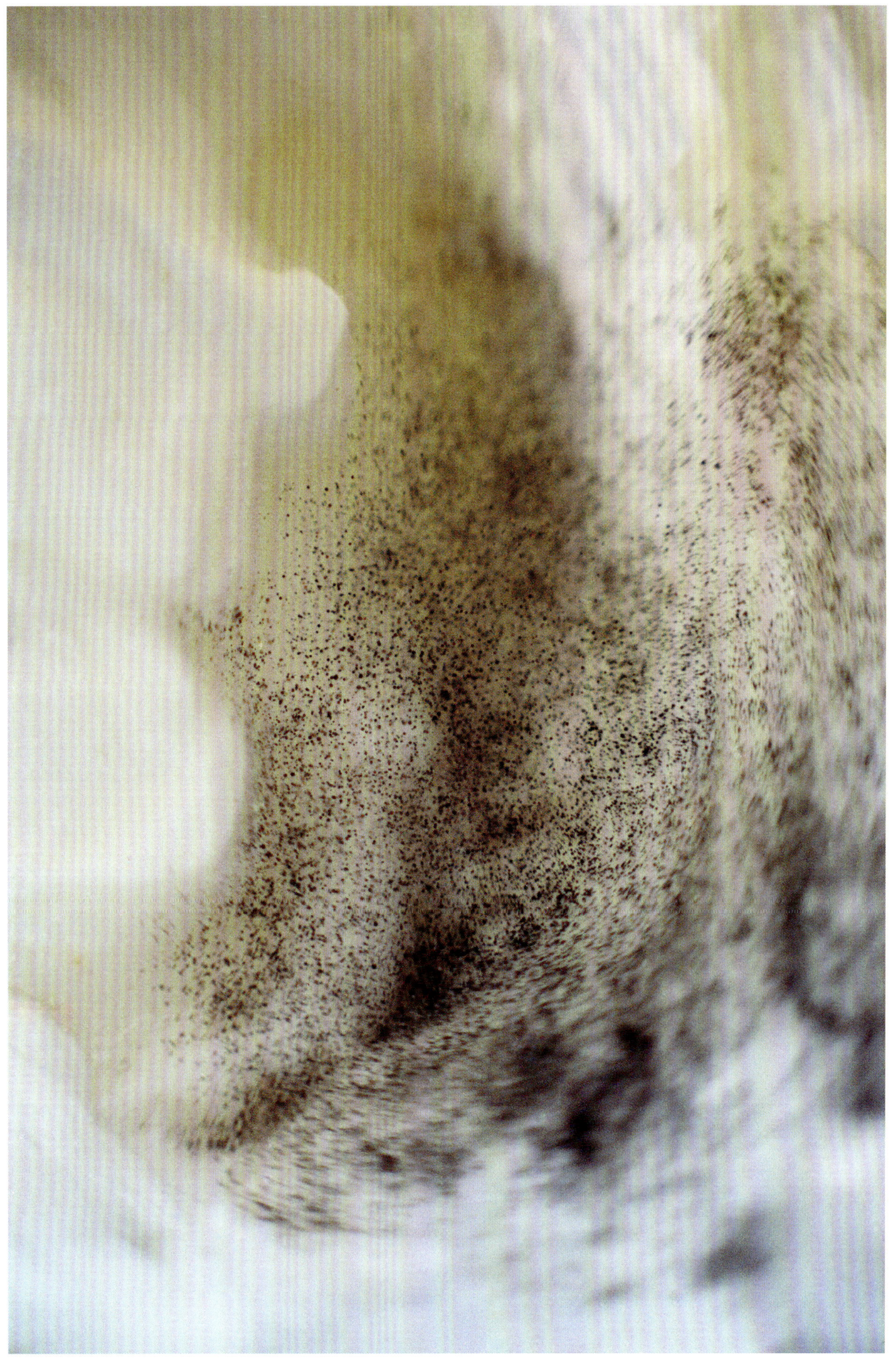

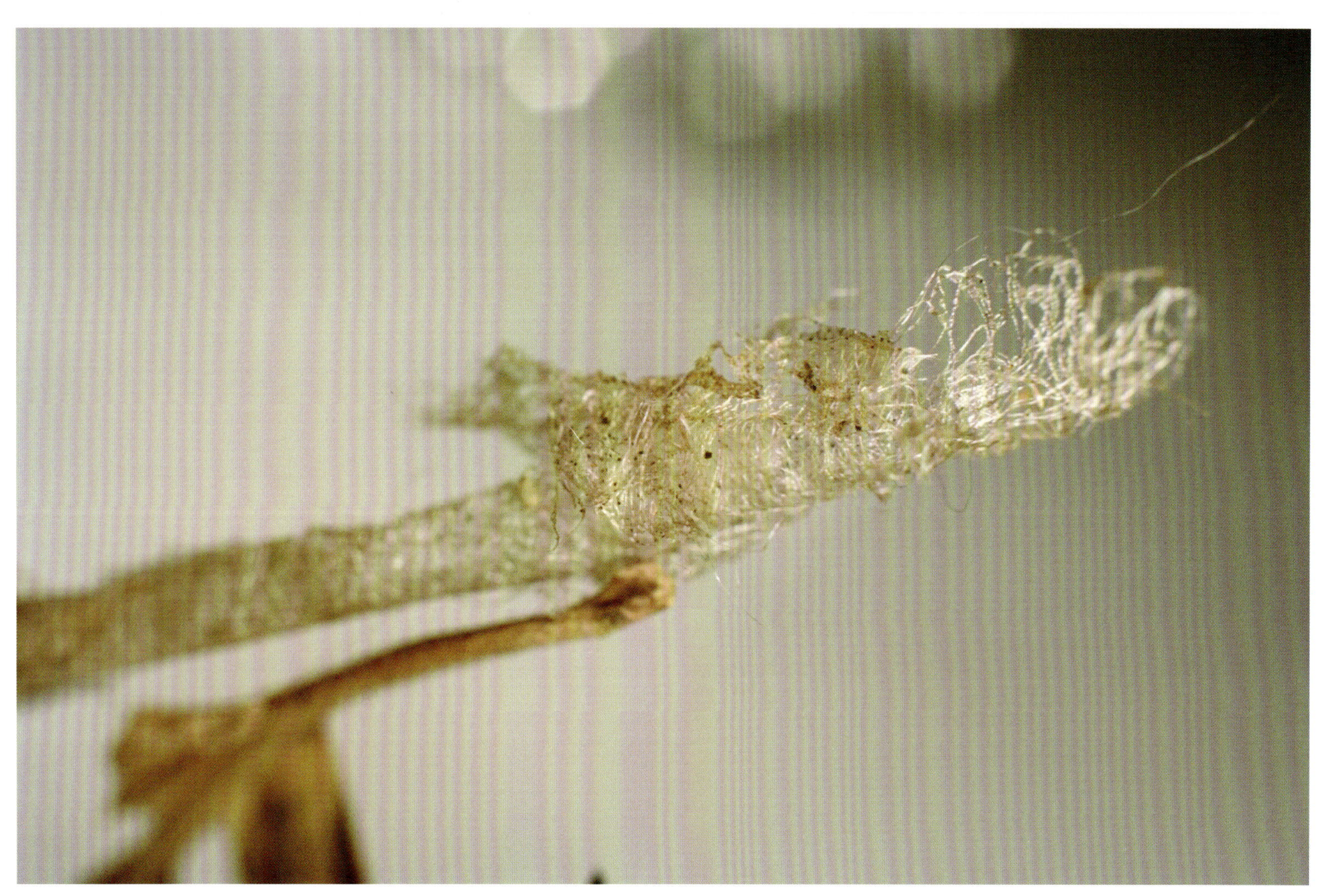

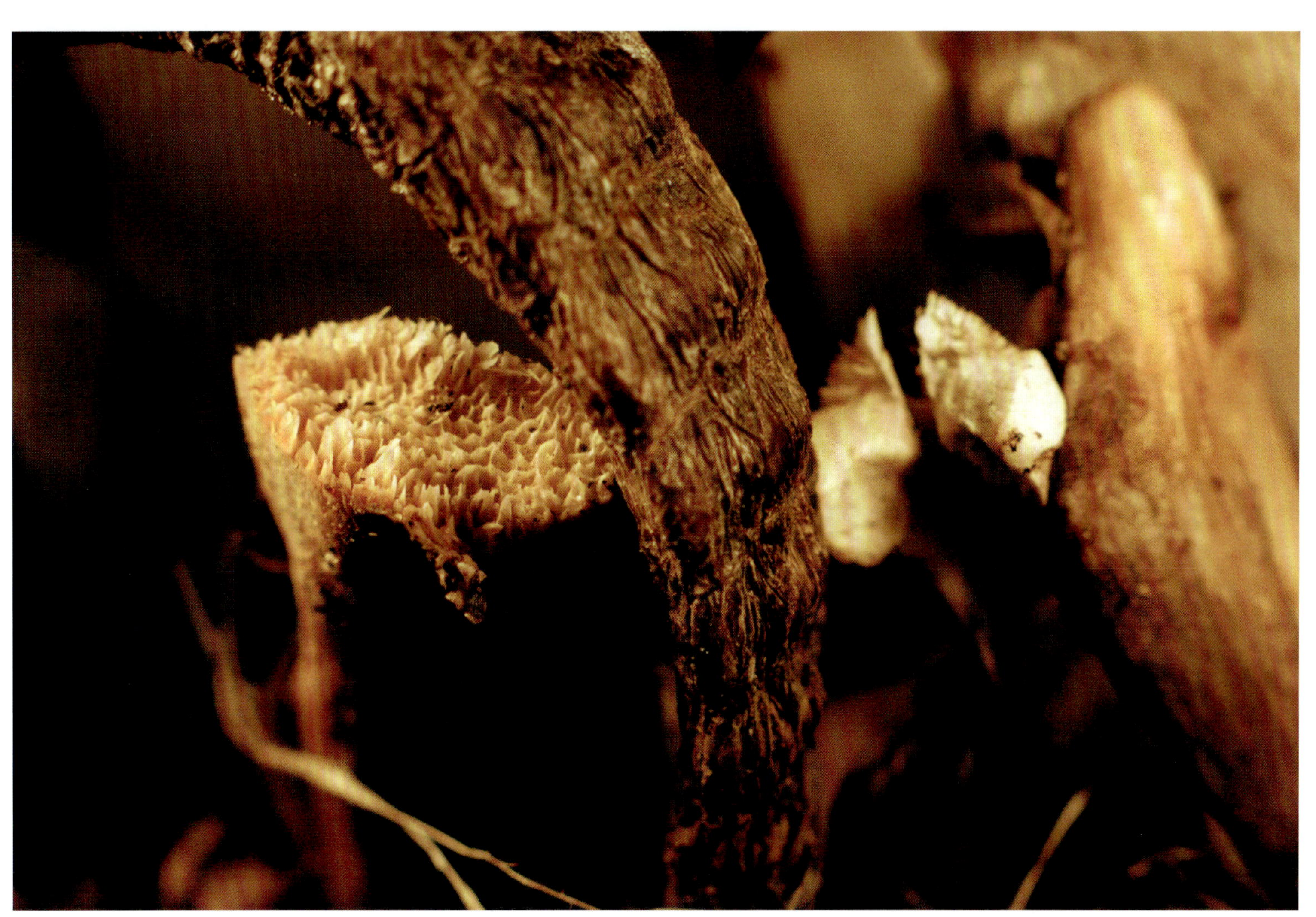

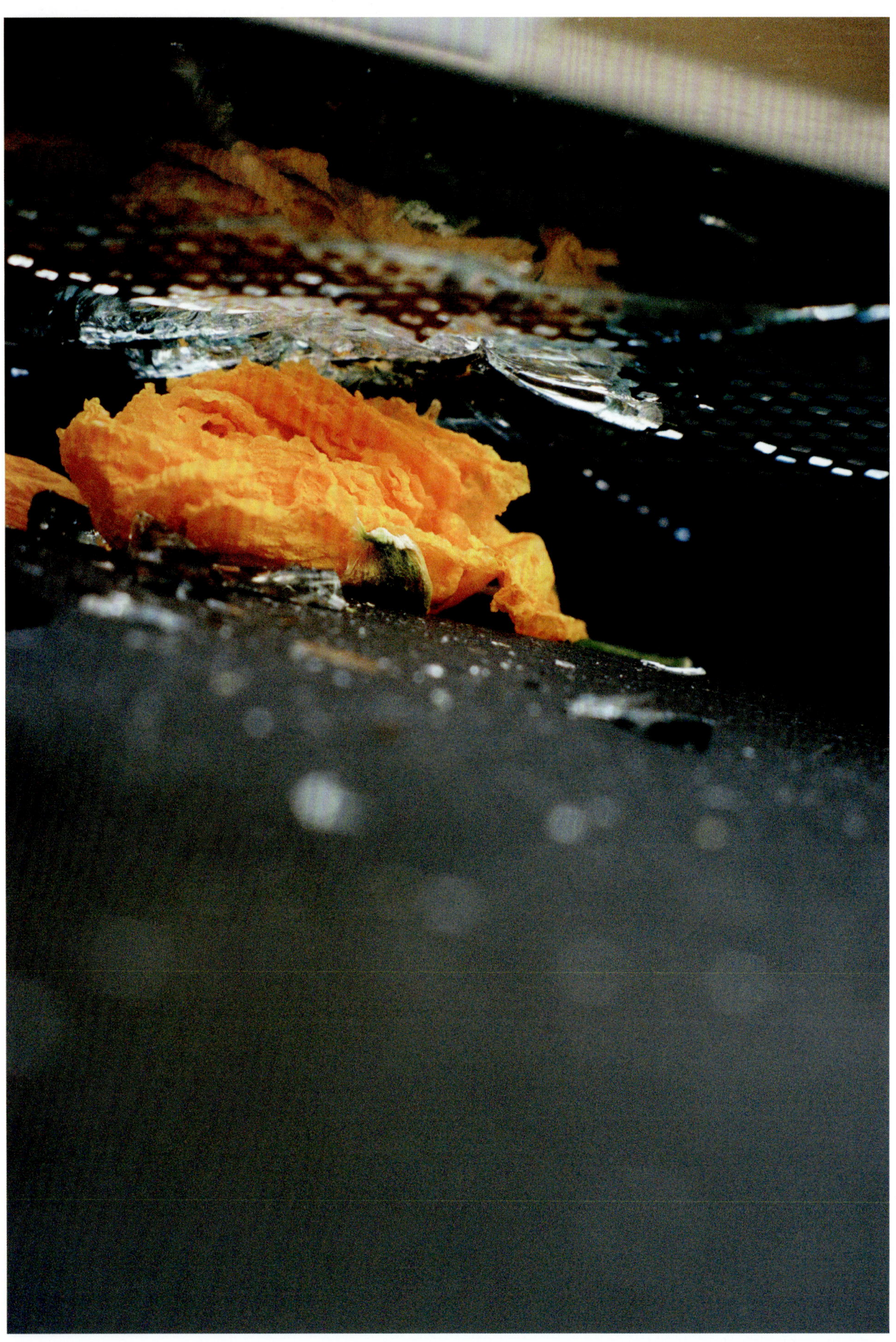

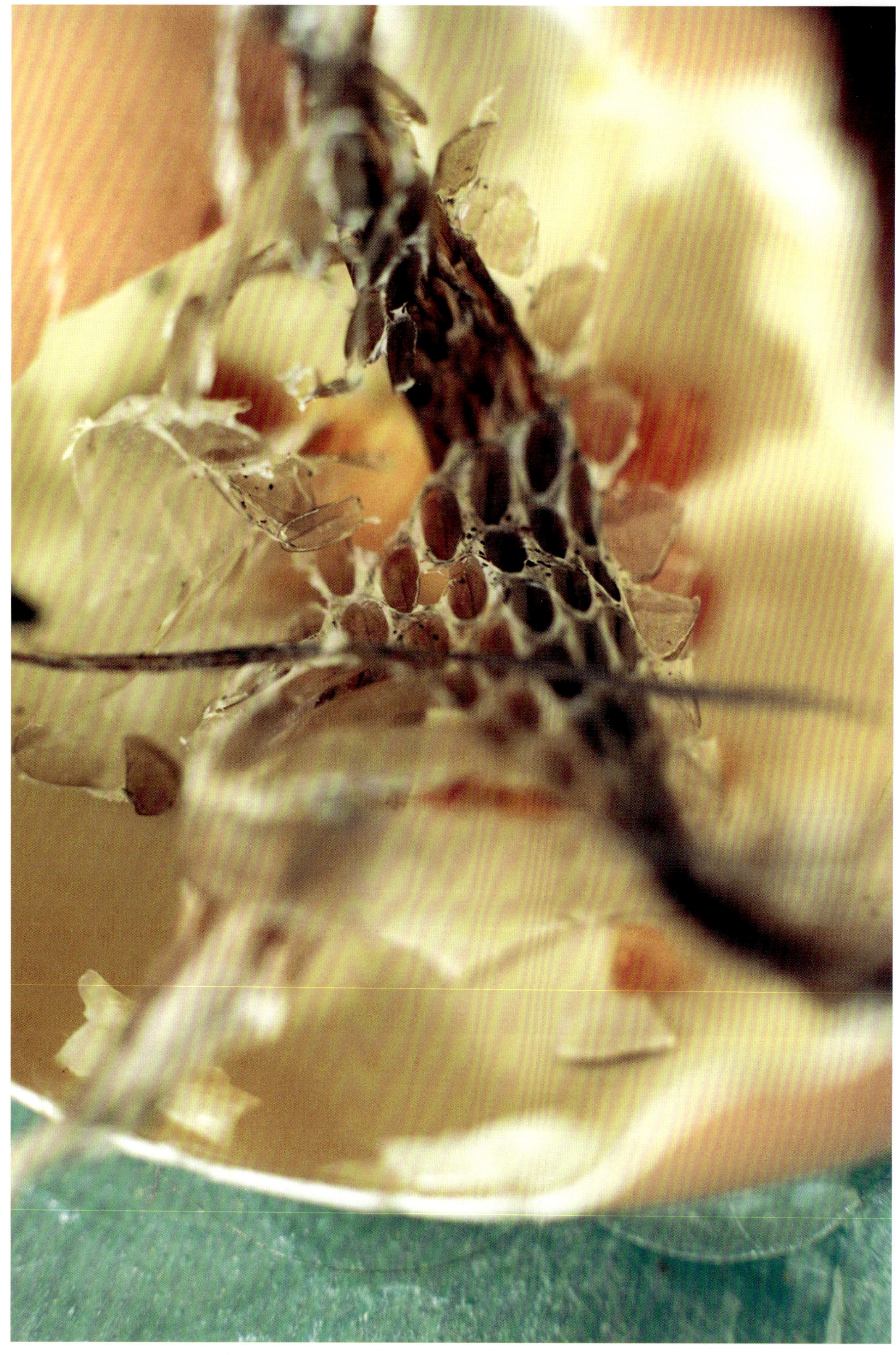

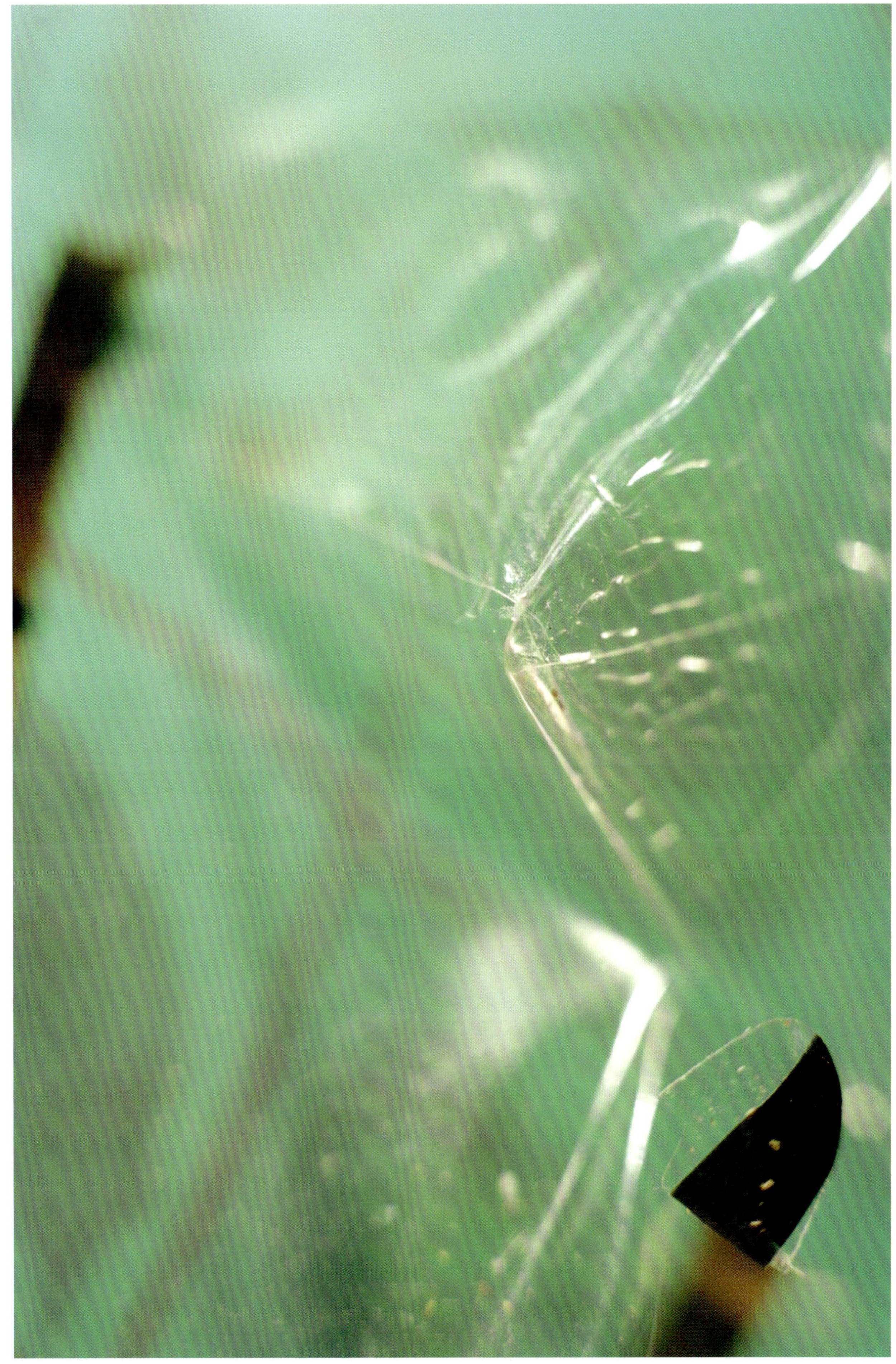

Postface

In early 2014, my father gave me a Polaroid camera that had been lying around his office unused for years and was set to be thrown out. The Polaroid Macro 5 was originally intended for dental and crime scene photography, but my own uses for the clunky device were unclear at first. Over the next few months, through experimentation and trial and error, a potential use gradually emerged. The camera quickly proved capable of capturing a feeling present in some of my (then) past images which I favored most, but I was not able to readily recreate. The prior images captured ordinary materials or subjects, but resulted in images that appear elusive and abstract—transformed by the staging, the framing and the process of being photographed.

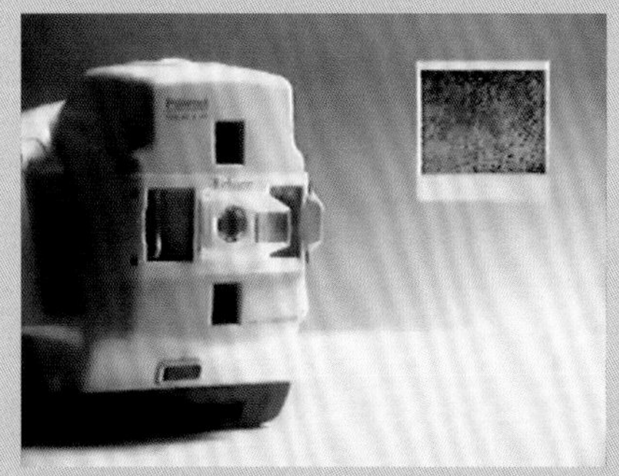

Developing the capacity to readily produce images of this nature led me to think more about the materials and the effects that I would ideally want these images to contain. The Macro 5 was particularly adept at capturing small objects at a close distance (specifically, 3 inches and 5 inches away from the camera's lens). I would incessantly scout for slight materials that looked like they'd make captivating and beguiling models. Toted around in film canisters and pill organizers, they'd come together in transient arrangements on an array of surfaces in my home. I eventually started to make comparable images with other cameras too, though images produced with each contained their own idiosyncratic style.

The images on the first few pages of this publication are some of the foundational images that document my initial acquaintance with this process. What follows are the results of somewhat divergent approaches: highly constructed, synthetic images and images of simpler models in more naturalistic arrangements. In different ways, both relay insular otherworldly landscapes full of almost-identifiable but inevitably indeterminate models of unknowable origin.

Index

All Photographs © Yair Oelbaum

Publication Design by Joey Engelhardt and Yair Oelbaum at P.I.P.
Finishing and Project Management by Kühle und Mozer
35mm Scans by Carl Saytor at Luxlab
Printed and bound by Kettler, Bönen

Enormous thanks to Kai Althoff and Dr. Victor Oelbaum
who (in different ways) paved the path that led to this book.

© 2024 Yair Oelbaum and
Verlag der Buchhandlung Walther und Franz König, Köln

Distribution by
Buchhandlung Walther König, Köln
T: +49-221-20596-53
verlag@buchhandlung-walther-koenig.de

UK & Eire
Cornerhouse Publications
HOME
2 Tony Wilson Place
UK Manchester M15 4FN
T: +44-161-2123466
publications@cornerhouse.org

Outside Europe
D.A.P. / Distributed Art Publishers, Inc.
75 Broad Street, Suite 630
USA New York, NY 10004
T: +1-212-627199
orders@dapinc.com

Printed in Germany

ISBN 978-3-7533-0581-3